£7.99

Annual Survey 2008

US Government & Politics

Anthony J. Bennett

Philip Allan Updates, an imprint of Hodder Education, part of Hachette Livre UK, Market Place, Deddington, Oxfordshire OX15 0SE

Orders
Bookpoint Ltd, 130 Milton Park, Abingdon, Oxfordshire OX14 4SB
tel: 01235 827720
fax: 01235 400454
e-mail: uk.orders@bookpoint.co.uk
Lines are open 9.00 a.m.–5.00 p.m., Monday to Saturday, with a 24-hour message answering service. You can also order through the Philip Allan Updates website: www.philipallan.co.uk

© Philip Allan Updates 2008

ISBN 978-1-84489-648-6

First published 2008
Impression number   5   4   3   2   1
Year   2013   2012   2011   2010   2009   2008

Printed by MPG Books, Bodmin

Hachette Livre UK's policy is to use papers that are natural, renewable and recyclable products and made from wood grown in sustainable forests. The logging and manufacturing processes are expected to conform to the environmental regulations of the country of origin.

Contents

Chapter 1

Primary chaos

There was a time when the 'invisible primary' was indeed invisible. When James Hadley first popularised the phrase in his 1976 book of that title, he described the invisible primary as a series of 'unnoticed manoeuvrings'. Around the same time, the highly esteemed political commentator of the *Washington Post*, David Broder, was telling us that 'nothing that happens before the first presidential primary has any relevance at all'. Things have changed dramatically in the last 30 years, and 2007 was the year of the not-so-invisible primary — a year packed with seemingly endless intra-party televised debates, as an enormous field of candidates on both sides slugged it out before the casting of any votes in a caucus or a primary.

Maybe it is the enormous number of candidates that has been one of the catalysts in making these usually invisible stages so visible this time around. The presidential election of 2008 will be the most open race for over half a century, for not since the election of 1952 has neither party fielded either an incumbent president or vice-president (see Table 1.1). This means that, for the first time in 14 elections, both parties have a genuinely open race.

Table 1.1 Incumbent presidents and vice-presidents running for the presidency, 1956–2004

Year	Incumbent running for the presidency	Party
1956	President Dwight Eisenhower	Republican
1960	Vice-President Richard Nixon	Republican
1964	President Lyndon Johnson	Democrat
1968	Vice-President Hubert Humphrey	Democrat
1972	President Richard Nixon	Republican
1976	President Gerald Ford	Republican
1980	President Jimmy Carter	Democrat
1984	President Ronald Reagan	Republican
1988	Vice-President George Bush	Republican
1992	President George Bush	Republican
1996	President Bill Clinton	Democrat
2000	Vice-President Al Gore	Democrat
2004	President George W. Bush	Republican

Declarations of intent started back in 2006, straight after that year's mid-term elections, with Democrat Congressman Dennis Kucinich of Ohio announcing his candidacy on 12 December 2006, followed 16 days later by former Senator John Edwards of North Carolina, who had been John Kerry's vice-presidential running mate in 2004. Within 2 months another 12 candidates jumped into the presidential race, making seven Democrats and seven Republicans (see Table 1.2). The only significant candidate to join the race after that was former Republican Senator Fred Thompson of Tennessee, who left it until 5 September 2007 to announce his candidacy. And in October, we had the first withdrawal, as Senator Sam Brownback bowed out.

Table 1.2 Presidential candidate announcements, by date

Date	Candidate	Party
2006		
12 December	Congressman Dennis Kucinich	Democrat
28 December	Ex-Senator John Edwards	Democrat
2007		
11 January	Congressman Ron Paul	Republican
	Senator Christopher Dodd	Democrat
20 January	Senator Hillary Clinton	Democrat
	Senator Sam Brownback (withdrew 19 October 2007)	Republican
	Governor Bill Richardson	Democrat
25 January	Congressman Duncan Hunter	Republican
28 January	Ex-Governor Mike Huckabee	Republican
31 January	Senator Joseph Biden	Democrat
5 February	Ex-Mayor Rudolph Giuliani	Republican
10 February	Senator Barack Obama	Democrat
14 February	Ex-Governor Mitt Romney	Republican
28 February	Senator John McCain	Republican
5 September	Ex-Senator Fred Thompson	Republican

In 2007, not only were there the candidate announcements to see — a traditional part of the 'invisible primary' — but much else besides. Televised presidential debates are normally held in the few weeks running up to the election itself, in September and October of election year. But 2007 witnessed no fewer than 16 Democrat debates and 12 Republican debates, as the field of candidates travelled from studio to studio and state to state, in a seemingly endless round of intra-party debates (see Table 1.3).

The events were mostly dull and predictable. In the Democratic debates, the big hitters — Senators Hillary Clinton and Barack Obama, and former Senator John Edwards — tried to ignore the also-rans. Obama caused something of a stir during a debate in July by promising, if elected, to meet the leaders of Iran,

Syria, Venezuela, Cuba and North Korea, without preconditions, during his first year in office. Clinton responded that she would not be asking these leaders to tea at the White House, and labelled Obama's response as naive. Senator Clinton had her own debate debacle later in the year, when she fluffed a question concerning illegal immigration. Meanwhile, the Republican big hitters — Rudy Giuliani, Mitt Romney and John McCain — had to put up with the libertarian views of Texas Congressman Ron Paul who, at least on the subject of Iraq, sounded more like a liberal Democrat than a member of the President's party.

Table 1.3 Presidential candidate-related events during 2007

Date	Event	Date	Event
26 April	Democratic debate	5 September	Republican debate
3 May	Republican debate	20 September	Democratic forum
15 May	Republican debate	26 September	Democratic debate
3 June	Democratic debate	27 September	Republican debate
5 June	Republican debate	14 October	Republican debate
28 June	Democratic debate	20 October	Democratic debate
23 July	Democratic debate	21 October	Republican debate
5 August	Republican debate	25 October	Republican forum
7 August	Democratic forum	30 October	Democratic debate
9 August	Democratic debate	6 November	Republican debate
11 August	Iowa straw poll	15 November	Democratic debate
19 August	Democratic forum	28 November	Republican debate
20 August	Republican forum	15 December	Democratic debate
22 August	Democratic forum	17 December	Democratic debate
23 August	Democratic forum		

More front loading

The presidential primaries and caucuses of 2008 started even earlier than in previous cycles, with the Iowa caucuses on 3 January and the New Hampshire primary on 8 January. This puts the voting in Iowa and New Hampshire — traditionally the first in the nation — 2 weeks earlier than in 2004.

Recent presidential nominating cycles have seen an ever-increasing trend towards 'front loading' — where states move their primaries and caucuses to the earlier part of the calendar, in order to increase the importance of these contests for their state. In 2008, front loading reached a new pitch, with 22 states scheduling their nominating contests on the first Tuesday in February (though in three states only the Democrats were holding a contest). These included states that had traditionally scheduled their primaries much later in the year. Between 2004 and 2008, for example, California moved up

from 2 March to 5 February, and Arkansas moved from mid-May to early February.

This stampede towards earlier voting can be seen in Table 1.4. Week –3 began on Monday 31 December. By 5 February 2008, 57% of the Democratic National Convention delegate votes and 55% of the Republican National Convention delegate votes were chosen. By the time of a similar date in 2000, the only states to have held their nomination votes were Iowa, Alaska and New Hampshire.

Eleven states are holding caucuses in 2008: Alaska, Colorado, Hawaii (Democrats), Iowa, Kansas (Republicans), Louisiana (Republicans), Maine, Minnesota, Nevada, North Dakota and Wyoming. As usual, these are mostly large states in terms of geography, but with small populations. All of these states (bar Louisiana and Minnesota) held caucuses in 2004.

Table 1.4 Number of presidential primaries held during each week of the primary season, 1988–2008

Week	1988	1992	1996	2000	2004	2008
–3	–	–	–	–	–	2
–2	–	–	–	–	–	1
–1	–	–	–	–	–	3
1	1	1	2	1	1	3
2	1	1	0	0	1	2
3	0	4	9	0	10	24
4	16	8	7	0	4	3
5	1	2	3	0	1	2
6	0	1	1	14	3	1
7	1	0	0	6	10	4
8	1	3	0	1	5	1
9	0	0	0	0	3	0
10	1	0	1	2	0	0
11	1	1	0	0	0	0
12	3	3	3	0	0	0
13	2	2	2	0	1	0
14	1	1	1	3	0	1
15	0	2	1	2	1	0
16	0	6	4	1	2	2
17	4	–	–	2	2	2
18	–	–	–	0	2	3
19	–	–	–	5	2	1
20	–	–	–	–	4	3

Different types of primaries

There are a number of different types of primary. They can vary by who is allowed to vote in them and by how delegates are then apportioned. In terms of who can vote in a primary, there are basically two different types: open and closed. In an **open primary**, any registered voter can choose to vote in either party's primary, though not in both. In a **closed primary**, only registered Republicans can vote in the Republican primary and only registered Democrats can vote in the Democratic primary. Most states hold closed primaries. Table 1.5 shows those states holding open primaries in 2008 (14 states in the Republican contest and 13 in the Democratic contest).

Table 1.5 States holding open primaries in 2008

Republican Party	Democratic Party
Alabama	Alabama
Arkansas	Arkansas
Idaho	Georgia
Illinois	Idaho
Indiana	Illinois
Michigan	Mississippi
Mississippi	Missouri
Missouri	Montana
Montana	Tennessee
Tennessee	Texas
Texas	Vermont
Vermont	Virginia
Virginia	Wisconsin
Wisconsin	

Table 1.6 States holding modified primaries in 2008

Republican Party	Democratic Party
Georgia	California
Maryland	Indiana
Massachusetts	Massachusetts
Nebraska	Michigan
New Hampshire	Nebraska
New Jersey	New Hampshire
North Carolina	New Jersey
Ohio	Ohio
Rhode Island	Rhode Island
Utah	South Carolina
West Virginia	Utah
	Washington
	West Virginia

Modified primaries also exist. These are like closed primaries, in that only registered party voters can vote, but it also allows those who have registered as independents to vote in either party's primary. So, for example, in the New Jersey presidential primary in 2008, registered Republican voters can vote only in the Republican primary, registered Democrat voters can vote only in the Democratic primary, but independent-registered voters can vote in either party's primary. In California in 2008, the Republican primary is closed, while the Democratic primary is modified, allowing independent voters to vote only in the Democratic primary, if they so wish. Table 1.6 shows states holding modified primaries in 2008 — 11 Republican primaries and 13 Democratic primaries.

Whether a state holds an open, closed or modified primary affects which candidates are likely to benefit. The more ideological candidates will do best in closed primaries, where only the party faithful can vote. But more moderate, 'centrist' or maverick candidates — such as Rudy Giuliani or John McCain — will tend to do better in open or modified primaries, where independent voters and even voters from the other party can participate.

Another kind of primary is related to the way delegates are apportioned. All Democratic primaries are **proportional primaries**. In other words, the number of delegates a candidate wins is proportional to the percentage of votes they win in the primary. States have a 15% minimum threshold and candidates who fail to reach that threshold gain no delegates at all.

However, many Republican primaries are **'winner-take-all' primaries**, where the candidate who wins the primary wins all the delegates from that state to the Republican National Convention. For example, whichever candidate wins the Republican primary in California will gain all of the state's 173 delegates. Other candidates will gain no delegates at all. In 2008, 16 state Republican parties, plus the District of Columbia, will hold a winner-take-all primary, representing 42% of the delegate votes at the Republican National Convention (see Table 1.7).

Table 1.7 Republican Party primary/caucus calendar, 2008

Month	Date	State	Election type	Delegates
January	Thursday 3	Iowa	Caucuses	40
	Saturday 5	Wyoming	Caucuses	14 (28)†
	Tuesday 8	New Hampshire	Primary	12 (24)†
	Tuesday 15	**Michigan**	***Primary**	**30 (60)†**
	Saturday 19	Nevada	Caucuses	34
		South Carolina	**Primary**	**24 (47)†**
	Tuesday 29	**Florida**	**Primary**	**57 (114)†**
February	Friday 1	Maine	Caucuses	21
	Tuesday 5	Alabama	*Primary	48
		Alaska	Caucuses	29
		Arizona	**Primary**	**53**
		Arkansas	*Primary	34
		California	**Primary**	**173**
		Colorado	Caucuses	46
		Connecticut	**Primary**	**30**
		Delaware	Primary	18
		Georgia	**Primary**	**72**
		Illinois	*Primary	70

Month	Date	State	Election type	Delegates
February *continued*	Tuesday 5	Massachusetts	Primary	43
		Minnesota	Caucuses	41
		Missouri	***Primary**	**58**
		New Jersey	Primary	52
		New York	**Primary**	**101**
		North Dakota	Caucuses	26
		Oklahoma	**Primary**	**41**
		Tennessee	*Primary	55
		Utah	Primary	36
	Saturday 9	Kansas	Caucuses	39
		Louisiana	Caucuses	46
	Tuesday 12	**District of Columbia**	**Primary**	**19**
		Maryland	**Primary**	**37**
		Virginia	***Primary**	**63**
	Tuesday 19	Washington	Primary	40
		Wisconsin	***Primary**	**40**
March	Tuesday 4	**Ohio**	**Primary**	**88**
		Rhode Island	Primary	20
		Texas	*Primary	140
		Vermont	***Primary**	**17**
	Tuesday 11	**Mississippi**	***Primary**	**39**
April	Tuesday 22	Pennsylvania	Primary	74
May	Tuesday 6	Indiana	*Primary	57
		North Carolina	Primary	69
	Tuesday 13	Nebraska	Primary	33
		West Virginia	Primary	30
	Tuesday 20	Kentucky	Primary	45
		Oregon	Primary	30
	Tuesday 27	Idaho	*Primary	32
June	Tuesday 3	Montana	*Primary	25
		New Mexico	Primary	32
		South Dakota	Primary	27

* Open Primary   † 50% of delegates lost as penalty for disobeying national party rules
Bold: Winner-take-all primary

Hawaii Republicans are not holding a primary or caucus (20 delegates). There are 59 additional delegates from US territories. Total number of delegates: 2,380 (or 2,516 without sanctions). Number of delegate votes required for nomination: 1,191 (or 1,259 without sanctions).

Table 1.8 Democratic Party primary/caucus calendar, 2008

Month	Date	State	Election type	Delegates
January	Thursday 3	Iowa	Caucuses	57
	Tuesday 8	New Hampshire	Primary	30
	Tuesday 15	Michigan	Primary	(156)†
	Saturday 19	Nevada	Caucuses	33
	Tuesday 29	Florida	Primary	(210)†
		South Carolina	Primary	54
February	Tuesday 5	Alabama	*Primary	60
		Alaska	Caucuses	18
		Arizona	Primary	67
		Arkansas	*Primary	47
		California	Primary	441
		Colorado	Caucuses	71
		Connecticut	Primary	60
		Delaware	Primary	23
		Georgia	*Primary	103
		Idaho	*Primary	23
		Illinois	*Primary	185
		Kansas	Caucuses	41
		Massachusetts	Primary	121
		Minnesota	Caucuses	88
		Missouri	*Primary	88
		New Jersey	Primary	127
		New Mexico	Primary	38
		New York	Primary	281
		North Dakota	Caucuses	21
		Oklahoma	Primary	47
		Tennessee	*Primary	85
		Utah	Primary	29
	Saturday 9	Louisiana	Primary	67
	Sunday 10	Maine	Caucuses	34
	Tuesday 12	District of Columbia	Caucuses	38
		Maryland	Primary	99
		Virginia	*Primary	101
	Tuesday 19	Hawaii	Caucuses	29
		Washington	Primary	97
		Wisconsin	*Primary	92

Month	Date	State	Election type	Delegates
March	Tuesday 4	Ohio	Primary	161
		Rhode Island	Primary	32
		Texas	*Primary	228
		Vermont	*Primary	23
	Saturday 8	Wyoming	Caucuses	18
	Tuesday 11	Mississippi	*Primary	40
April	Tuesday 22	Pennsylvania	Primary	188
May	Tuesday 6	Indiana	Primary	85
		North Carolina	Primary	134
	Tuesday 13	Nebraska	Primary	31
		West Virginia	Primary	39
	Tuesday 20	Kentucky	Primary	60
		Oregon	Primary	65
June	Tuesday 3	Montana	*Primary	24
		South Dakota	Primary	23

*Open Primary
† All delegates forfeited for disobeying national party rules

Kansas Democrats are not holding a primary or caucus (41 delegates). There are 99 delegates from US territories. Total number of delegates: 4,051. Number of delegate votes required for nomination: 2,026.

A flawed process

The 2008 primaries have shown the nomination process to be out of control and fundamentally flawed. In the months leading up to the primaries, there was an unseemly stampede by state parties to move earlier in the nominating calendar, with some state parties openly flouting the rules set by the national parties. Forty years after the old nominating system — dominated by party bosses in smoke-filled rooms — was blown to pieces, the system that replaced it has all but collapsed in chaos. What it has left us with is a 5 February national primary in all but name, and a national primary arrived at not as a result of deliberation, but as a consequence of a political free-for-all. This is the year of primary chaos.

The free-for-all became evident when Florida Democrats moved their primary to 29 January 2008 (see Table 1.8). The Democratic Party's National Committee rules for the selection of delegates to the party's National Convention in 2008 stated that only Iowa, New Hampshire, Nevada and South Carolina could hold primaries or caucuses before 5 February 2008. In response to the decision by Florida Democrats, the Democratic National Committee voted in August 2007 to strip the Florida Democratic Party of all

its 210 national convention delegates, unless the party moved its primary back to 5 February. On 23 September, the Florida Democratic Party responded by stating that it was keeping its January primary. In a statement, the chair of the Florida Democratic Party, Karen Thurman, explained the reason for the decision:

> There will be no other primary [on that day]. The nation will be paying attention, and Florida Democrats will have a major impact in determining who the next President of the United States of America will be.

Florida Democrats applauded the decision, but it highlighted the crisis in the presidential nominating process. In December 2007, the Democratic National Committee stripped Michigan of all its 156 delegates for the same reason.

In late October 2007, the chair of the Republican National Committee (RNC), Mike Duncan, imposed a 50% cut in the number of delegates allocated to New Hampshire, South Carolina, Florida, Michigan and Wyoming, as a penalty for those state Republican parties scheduling their primaries before the sanctioned date. 'It's very important that our party uphold and enforce the rules that we unanimously voted into place at the Republican National Convention in 2004,' said Duncan. His decision was endorsed by the full RNC on 8 November, by 121 votes to 9. The state parties vowed to fight the sanction through the courts.

The *National Journal* asked its political insiders the following question: 'All things considered, is the front loading of the 2008 presidential nominating process a good or bad development?' In response, 69% of Democrats and 71% of Republicans believed that it was a bad development. Among the comments that these veteran politicians made were:

> The front loading of the process anoints money as the most important variable needed to secure victory.

> Too little time to really evaluate the candidates.

> The [traditional] calendar tested a candidate's endurance, organisation, message and personal mettle in a way that was better preparation for the job than the truncated, money-driven, 'one-show, goodbye' national primary day we are creating.

> This is madness. Now, if you don't have $80 million, you have no chance whatsoever. There is no time for the ebb and flow of momentum, and no real time for voters to vet the candidates.

Professor Linda Fowler of Dartmouth College agreed. Writing in *Newsday* in May 2007, she had this to say:

> No longer will candidates have a chance to experiment with themes that may resonate with the electorate and build momentum state by state. The edge

will go more to candidates able to most successfully court donors and activists in what insiders call the 'invisible primary'. The idea of a candidate using Iowa and New Hampshire to bring new life and new ideas to the party establishment will be a thing of the past. Perhaps I would feel better about squeezing the last vestiges of democracy from presidential elections if the change had occurred with some thought about the results rather than raw political calculation.

In September 2007, the *New York Times* published an editorial under the heading 'The Primary Problem'. It reached much the same conclusion:

> The presidential primary system is broken. This Wild West approach could make the primary season absurdly early. States keep leapfrogging backward over each other until their primaries were scheduled in the winter of the year before the general election.

Katherine Seelye, also writing in the *New York Times* ('Volatile Primary Calendar Poses Hazards for Groups', 20 September 2007), described the primary election calendar as 'a shambles'. Everyone agrees that something must be done to repair the damage to the nominating process before 2012. There are many reform proposals being circulated, but it will take cooperation between the two national parties to secure meaningful reform. And so, concluded the *New York Times* editorial (2 September 2007):

> The two parties should begin a discussion of the best reform proposals now, and plan on having a new system in place for 2012. The presidential nominating process is too important to American democracy to be allowed to descend into gamesmanship and chaos.

The trouble is that agreement has to be made between the 50 state parties, many of which are the ones who have contributed to this year's primary chaos. The presidential nominating system has never been an orderly process, but this year's fiasco reinforces many Americans' view that the political system is broken.

The Democrat candidates

As election year dawns, there are three front-runner candidates in the race for the Democratic presidential nomination — or perhaps more accurately two front-runners and another following at a distance. It is nearly 50 years since Americans elected a sitting US Senator to the presidency — the last was John F. Kennedy in 1960. Others tried — George McGovern (1972) and John Kerry (2004) — but failed. The Democrats' last two successful candidates were both former state Governors, Jimmy Carter of Georgia (1976) and Bill Clinton of Arkansas (1992). However, this year's front-runners are two serving Senators and one former Senator: Hillary Clinton of New York, Barack Obama of Illinois and John Edwards of North Carolina.

Another surprise about these three candidates is how little real political experience they have. At the start of 2008, these three had only 16 years of Senate service between them: Clinton 7 years, Edwards 6 years and Obama 3 years. In contrast, at the start of 2004, John Kerry (that year's Democratic presidential candidate) had already served 18 years in the Senate. Many commentators attribute more 'experience' to Hillary Clinton, adding in her 8 years as First Lady, but this can hardly be classified as political experience. What is more, the only time President Bill Clinton gave his wife a role in policy making — healthcare reform legislation — it was an unmitigated disaster.

Hillary Clinton	Barack Obama	John Edwards
■ Born: 26 October 1947.	■ Born: 4 August 1961.	■ Born: 10 June 1953.
■ Age on election day: 61.	■ Age on election day: 47.	■ Age on election day: 55.
■ Lived mostly in: Illinois, Arkansas, Washington DC, New York.	■ Lived mostly in: Hawaii, Jakarta (Indonesia), Illinois.	■ Lived mostly in: North Carolina.
■ Profession: lawyer.	■ Profession: lawyer.	■ Profession: lawyer.
■ Church affiliation: Methodist.	■ Church affiliation: United Church of Christ.	■ Church affiliation: Methodist.
■ First Lady: 1993–2001.	■ Elected to the US Senate (Illinois): 2004.	■ Elected to the US Senate (North Carolina): 1998; served one term.
■ Elected to the US Senate (New York): 2000; re-elected 2006.	■ Years of service in elective politics as of January 2008: 11 (8 in Illinois State Senate).	■ Democratic vice-presidential candidate: 2004.
■ Years of service in elective politics as of January 2008: 7.		■ Years of service in elective politics as of January 2008: 6.

It is a first to have a woman as a front-running candidate for a major party's presidential nomination. It is over 40 years since Senator Margaret Chase Smith of Maine ran for the Republican party's presidential nomination in 1964, finishing second in the final ballot to Barry Goldwater. In 1972, Representative Shirley Chisholm of New York became the first Democrat woman (and the first African-American) to seek the presidency. Republican Elizabeth Dole in 2000 and Democrat Carol Moseley Braun in 2004 each made brief and unsuccessful bids for their party's presidential nomination.

There are plenty of examples of the electorate voting for the complete opposite of the current incumbent. After 8 years of the grandfatherly Eisenhower, Americans elected the youthful Kennedy. After the lies of consummate Washington-insider Richard Nixon, they elected Jimmy Carter, the candidate who said 'I'll never lie to you', but who had no Washington experience at all. After the sleazy Bill Clinton who could (and did) smooth-talk his way out of anything, Americans elected a born-again Christian who had a tenuous grasp of policy detail and who used words like 'misunderestimate' and 'strategery' —

George W. Bush. One might have thought that 2008 would be the year of the policy expert with decades of political experience — someone like Al Gore, the former vice-president and unsuccessful presidential candidate in 2000. Instead, Americans seem destined to pick a president who boasts little if any federal government experience.

The Republican candidates

Whereas the Democratic race for the presidency produced a clear and early front-runner in Hillary Clinton, the Republican race was confused and unclear throughout 2007. For most of the year there were three leading candidates — Rudy Giuliani of New York, John McCain of Arizona and Mitt Romney of Massachusetts — joined by a fourth, Fred Thompson of Tennessee. It is a motley bunch: a former city mayor, a veteran Senator, a former state Governor and an ex-Senator-turned-actor. Only McCain and Thompson have Washington experience, but only Giuliani and Romney have executive experience. By November 2007, this foursome had been joined by a fifth candidate, Mike Huckabee — another former state Governor.

At the beginning of 2007, Senator John McCain was the undisputed front-runner. McCain lost in the primaries to George W. Bush in 2000, but now it seemed to be 'his turn'. Back in 2000, McCain had run an insurgent campaign, attracting votes from independents and Democrats in open primary states, and he was the favourite of the political press corps. McCain had travelled round America on his 'Straight Talk Express' bus, the press hanging on his every word. Seven years later, it all seemed rather tired and bland. By the summer, McCain was falling behind badly in fundraising and in the polls. His biggest difficulty was in his wholesale backing of the unpopular war in Iraq and the President's policies for that country.

That gave an opening to Rudy Giuliani and Mitt Romney. Giuliani has obvious advantages and disadvantages in trying to be chosen as the Republican presidential candidate. On the plus side, many Americans of both parties admire the role he played as Mayor of New York City on 11 September 2001. He became, as it were, 'America's mayor'. People also respect the fact that under his watch, the streets of New York became safer. Anyone who can get elected as a Republican in New York City must be able to attract independent and Democrat voters. However, on the negative side, Giuliani has a colourful private life, a fierce temper, and views on key issues — abortion and gay rights, for example — that sit uncomfortably with many Republicans, let alone the more conservative voters who tend to turn up at primaries. Giuliani's only hope is that Republicans come to see him, not as the candidate they really wanted, but the only one on offer with a chance of defeating Hillary Clinton. Towards the end of 2007, Giuliani was much stronger in head-to-head polls with Senator Clinton than either Fred Thompson or Mitt Romney.

John McCain

- Born: 29 August 1936.
- Age on election day: 72.
- Lived mostly in: Arizona.
- Profession: US Navy; decorated for service in Vietnam.
- Church affiliation: Baptist.
- Elected to the US Senate (Arizona): 1986.
- Years of service in elective politics as of January 2008: 21.

Rudy Giuliani

- Born: 28 May 1944.
- Age on election day: 64.
- Lived mostly in: New York.
- Profession: lawyer.
- Church affiliation: Roman Catholic.
- Elected Mayor of New York City: 1993.
- Years of service in elective politics as of January 2008: 8.

Mitt Romney

- Born: 12 March 1947.
- Age on election day: 61.
- Lived mostly in: Michigan, Massachusetts.
- Profession: businessman.
- Church affiliation: Mormon.
- Elected Governor of Massachusetts: 2002; served one term.
- Years of service in elective politics as of January 2008: 4.

Fred Thompson

- Born: 19 August 1942.
- Age on election day: 66.
- Lived mostly in: Alabama, Tennessee.
- Profession: lawyer, actor.
- Church affiliation: Church of Christ.
- Elected to the US Senate (Tennessee): 1994; served part-term and one full term.
- Years of service in elective politics as of January 2008: 8.

Mike Huckabee

- Born: 24 August 1955.
- Age on election day: 53.
- Lived mostly in: Arkansas.
- Profession: Baptist minister.
- Church affiliation: Southern Baptist.
- Served as Governor of Arkansas: 1996–2007.
- Years of service in elective politics as of January 2008: 14.

The former Massachusetts governor Mitt Romney is presenting himself as someone who has a wide appeal. He was elected as a Republican Governor in what must be the Democratic Party's safest state. He has portrayed himself as Mr Competence — someone with proven executive skills. But Romney, too, has faults. The main problem may be his religion: he is a Mormon, a religious sect that many Americans regard with suspicion. Would evangelical Christians vote in large numbers for a Mormon candidate? Only if Romney can convince them that he, and only he, can defeat their nemesis, Hillary Clinton.

It is extraordinary that only one of the four leading Republicans can suggest that they come from the conservative side of the party. Giuliani and Romney are both moderate/liberal and McCain is regarded as a maverick. Fred Thompson tries to portray himself as the natural heir to the party of Ronald Reagan. Like Reagan, Thompson is an actor-turned-politician. He plays New York City District Attorney Arthur Branch in the NBC television series *Law and Order*. He has appeared in more than 20 films, including *The Hunt for Red October* (1990) and *Bury My Heart at Wounded Knee* (2007), where he played President Ulysses Grant. Thompson left his announcement very late — almost 9 months after most other candidates — announcing his candidacy only on

5 September 2007. Such a late start is a huge drawback in terms of raising money and putting together an effective, nationwide organisation.

The dark horse candidate is Mike Huckabee, hardly seen in the polls or talked about in the media until late in 2007. Of the five leading Republican candidates, Huckabee looks most like a typical Republican presidential candidate. Unlike McCain, Giuliani and Romney, Huckabee is from the south and is seen as a safe conservative. He was born in Hope, Arkansas, and has served as that state's Governor. His conservative credentials are bolstered by being a Baptist minister, someone with whom evangelical Christians (an important constituency for the Republican Party) feel comfortable. Huckabee is by far the youngest of the Republican candidates — he will be 53 on election day.

How could the Democrats win in 2008?

The result of the 2004 presidential election was notable for its similarity to the result 4 years earlier. Only two states changed hands: New Mexico switched from the Democrats to the Republicans and New Hampshire switched from the Republicans to the Democrats. In 2000, George W. Bush won by 271–267 electoral college votes, and in 2004 he won by 286–252. The Democrats were thus just 18 electoral votes short of victory in 2004.

Which states might the Democrats hope to pick up to win the White House? There are five so-called red (Republican) states that could switch to the blue (Democrat) column in 2008. Four are desert southwest and Rocky Mountain states: Arizona, Nevada, New Mexico and Colorado. The other is Virginia. Four of these five states have Democrat Governors, whereas in 2000 all five states had Republican Governors. Four of these five states have one Democrat Senator and only Arizona has two Republican Senators. Back in 2000, Colorado and Virginia also had two Republican Senators. In three of these states, a Republican Senator is retiring in 2008: Wayne Allard in Colorado, Pete Domenici in New Mexico and John Warner in Virginia. The Democrats have high hopes of picking up all three open seats (see Chapter 7).

Arizona used to be a solid Republican state. It has voted for the Republican candidate for the White House in 13 of the last 14 elections, only voting Democrat in 1996 to re-elect Bill Clinton. The Democrats picked up two of the state's House seats in the 2006 mid-term elections. Likewise Virginia: again, 13 out of 14 elections in the Republican column, breaking the trend only in 1964 to re-elect Lyndon Johnson. Colorado has voted Republican in 12 of the last 14 elections, voting Democrat only in 1964 (re-electing Johnson) and 1992 (electing Bill Clinton). The Democrats picked up one of the state's House seats in 2006. These states are tending more to the Democrat column and between them they command 42 electoral college votes. Winning just two or three of them (while holding on to their 2004 states) would give a Democrat candidate victory in 2008. Other battleground states are likely to be Florida, Iowa and Ohio, all narrowly won by the Republicans in 2004. There are another 54 electoral college votes for those states. Add Missouri's 11 electoral votes, and one can see that there are plenty of states in play to make 2008 a real chance for the Democrats.

Finally, the Democrats might also be mindful of the fact that only once since 1880 has a president who had served two full terms been succeeded by someone of the same party, when Ronald Reagan was succeeded by the first George Bush in 1988.

Questions

1 Why can 2007 be viewed as the year of the not-so-invisible primary?
2 When was the last time a presidential election was held in which no incumbent president or vice-president ran as a candidate?
3 Who was the first candidate to declare his presidential nomination for 2008, and on what date did he do this?
4 Explain the term 'front loading'. Why does this occur?
5 What percentage of National Party Convention delegates will have been chosen by 5 February 2008?
6 How many states are holding caucuses in 2008? Give two examples.
7 Explain the differences between (a) open primaries, (b) closed primaries and (c) modified primaries.
8 Explain the difference between (a) proportional primaries and (b) winner-take-all primaries.
9 What evidence is there for 2008 being a 'free-for-all' in fixing primary and caucus dates? What happened in Florida?
10 Use the extracts from Professor Linda Fowler and the *New York Times* to write a short paragraph outlining the problems with the candidate selection process in 2008.
11 What is different about the amount of political experience possessed by Democrat candidates in 2008 and that of John Kerry in 2004?
12 What are the advantages and disadvantages that Rudy Giuliani faces in trying to win the Republican presidential nomination?
13 What is Mitt Romney's principal advantage and disadvantage?
14 Which states do the Democrats hope to win in 2008 that George W. Bush won in 2004?

Chapter 2

Membership of the 110th Congress

What you need to know

- Congress is the legislative branch of the federal government.
- It is made up of two houses: the House of Representatives and the Senate.
- A Congress lasts for 2 years.
- The Congress meeting from January 2007 to January 2009 is the 110th Congress; the first Congress met from 1789 to 1791.
- The membership of the 110th Congress was largely decided by the mid-term congressional elections held in November 2006.
- In these elections, the Democrats won control of both houses of Congress for the first time in 12 years.

The 110th Congress began its business at the beginning of January 2007. For the first time in 12 years, both houses were controlled by the Democrats. This meant that all the leadership positions (such as House Speaker, majority and minority leaders, as well as all committee chairmanships) changed in terms of personnel. Democrats now held the House speakership, the majority leader posts in both houses as well as the chairmanships of all House and Senate committees and subcommittees.

Party balance

In the Senate, the matter of party balance is more complicated than before. At the end of the 109th Congress, the Democrats held just 44 of the 100 Senate seats. The Republicans held 55 and there was one independent — James Jeffords of Vermont — who, although elected as a Republican in 2000, tended to vote with the Democrats.

In the 2006 mid-term elections, the Republicans lost six seats: Missouri, Montana, Ohio, Pennsylvania, Rhode Island and Virginia. That reduced their number in the Senate to just 49. The Democrats gained six seats — those named above — but effectively lost one. Joe Lieberman of Connecticut, the incumbent Democrat, lost the Senate Democratic primary. But in the general election, the official Democrat candidate, Ned Lamont, gained only 40% of the vote, with Lieberman — running as an independent — gaining 50%. Lieberman thus returned to the Senate, now sitting as an independent, though he aligns himself with Senate Democrats.

The one remaining seat — the Vermont seat formerly held by independent James Jeffords — is still independent following the election of former House member Bernie Sanders. Sanders, like Lieberman, caucuses with the Democrats. So the actual party balance in the Senate is 49 Democrats, 49 Republicans and 2 independents. However, the effective party balance is 51 Democrats and 49 Republicans.

Wyoming Senator Craig Thomas died of leukaemia on 5 June 2007 at the age of 74. Thomas was elected to the House in 1989 in a special election to replace Dick Cheney, who had just been appointed Secretary of Defense by (the first) President Bush. Thomas was then elected to the Senate in 1994 and re-elected in 2000 and 2006. He won his most recent election with 70% of the vote. Thomas was the first Senator to die in office for almost 5 years. Senator Paul Wellstone (Democrat–Minnesota) died in October 2002. In total, eight Senators have died in office since 1987.

Wyoming state law mandates that the state Governor must nominate a replacement from the same party as the deceased member. This fact is of significance, as the governorship of Wyoming in the middle of 2007 was held by a Democrat, Dave Freudenthal. The state's Republican Party presented the Governor with a list of three possible nominees, from which he had to select one. On Friday 22 June, just 17 days after Senator Thomas's death, the Wyoming Governor appointed John Barrasso, a Republican state Senator, to fill the vacancy until a special election in November 2008. Barrasso has already announced that he will be a candidate in that special election to serve out the remaining 4 years of Thomas's 6-year term. This will result in two Senate races taking place in Wyoming in 2008: one for the remainder of Thomas's term and the scheduled one (the other Wyoming Senator, Mike Enzi, will have completed his 6-year term by then). John Barrasso, formerly an orthopaedic surgeon, was elected to the Wyoming state senate in 2002 and had a conservative voting record during his 5 years there. In that respect, he will tread much the same ideological path as his predecessor.

In the House, the party balance is currently 233 Democrats and 202 Republicans, with no independent members. At the end of the 109th Congress, the Republicans held 232 seats and the Democrats 202, with one independent who caucused with the Democrats, making the effective party balance 232 Republicans and 203 Democrats. The Republicans lost 30 seats in the mid-term elections, thereby reducing their number to 202. The Democrats picked up 30 seats from the Republicans, plus the one independent seat in Vermont.

Ideological patterns

In Congress, however, party labels do not necessarily mean voting together. Conservative Democrats, like Congressman Gene Taylor of Mississippi or

Senator Mary Landrieu of Louisiana, often vote with Republicans. Likewise, moderate Republicans, such as Congressman Christopher Shays of Connecticut or Senator Olympia Snowe of Maine, often vote with Democrats.

Table 2.1 shows the most conservative Democrat and moderate Republican members of each house during 2006. This makes clear the geographic and regional basis of political ideology in American politics. Eight of the ten most conservative Democrat House members come from the south, as do four of the five most conservative Democrat Senators. Eight of the ten most moderate Republican House members come from either the northeast or the upper mid-west, as do three of the five most moderate Republican Senators. Nine of the ten most conservative Democrat House members come from states that George W. Bush won in both 2000 and 2004, as do all the five most conservative Democrat Senators. Finally, eight of the ten most moderate Republican House members come from states won by Al Gore in 2000 and by John Kerry in 2004, as do all the five most moderate Republican Senators.

Table 2.1 Most conservative Democrat and moderate Republican members of Congress

Most conservative Democrat House members	Most moderate Republican House members
Dan Boren (Oklahoma)	Christopher Shays (Connecticut)
Jim Marshall (Georgia)	Walter Jones (North Carolina)
Gene Taylor (Mississippi)	Wayne Gilchrest (Maryland)
Henry Cuellar (Texas)	Jim Ramstad (Minnesota)
Collin Peterson (Minnesota)	Chris Smith (New Jersey)
Bud Cramer (Alabama)	Vernon Ehlers (Michigan)
John Barrow (Georgia)	Michael Castle (Delaware)
Charlie Melancon (Louisiana)	Jim Gerlach (Pennsylvania)
Lincoln Davis (Tennessee)	Jeff Flake (Arizona)
Jim Matheson (Utah)	Mark Kirk (Illinois)
Most conservative Democrat Senators	**Most moderate Republican Senators**
Ben Nelson (Nebraska)	Olympia Snowe (Maine)
Mary Landrieu (Louisiana)	Susan Collins (Maine)
Mark Pryor (Arkansas)	Arlen Specter (Pennsylvania)
Bill Nelson (Florida)	Norm Coleman (Minnesota)
Blanche Lincoln (Arkansas)	Gordon Smith (Oregon)

Source: *National Journal*, 3 March 2007, pp. 32–33

It is also interesting in the Senate to note how the two Senators from each state vote — to what extent they have similar or different voting records. After all, because they are representing the same constituents, you might expect them to vote quite similarly. However, this is not always the case. In a recent analysis on voting behaviour during 2006, the *National Journal* (3 March 2007) referred to Senators from the same state as falling into the categories of either

'twins' — those with very similar voting records — or 'odd couples'; the 'odd couples' could be either of different parties or the same (see Table 2.2).

The two same-state Senators who vote most alike are the two Republicans from Georgia, Saxby Chambliss and Johnny Isakson, followed by the two New Jersey Democrats, Frank Lautenberg and Bob Menendez. These two sets of same-state, same-party Senators are political identical twins. In the first 207 roll-call votes in the Senate in 2007, Chambliss and Isakson voted together on 202 of the votes (98%) and Lautenberg and Menendez voted together on 201 (97%).

The two same-state Senators who vote most differently are Charles Grassley (R) and Tom Harkin (D) of Iowa. Grassley is a conservative Republican and Harkin a liberal Democrat. In the first 207 roll-call votes in 2007, Grassley and Harkin voted together on only 101 of them (49%). In much the same position are Pete Domenici (R) and Jeff Bingaman (D) of New Mexico. These really are same-state 'odd couples'.

The two same-state, *same party* Senators who vote most differently are the two Arizonan Republicans, John McCain and Jon Kyl. Kyl has a conservative voting record, while McCain operates as what might be described as 'a moderate maverick'.

Table 2.2 Senate 'twins' and 'odd couples'

Same-state Senators with most similar voting records
Saxby Chambliss and Johnny Isakson (R–Georgia)
Frank Lautenberg and Bob Menendez (D–New Jersey)
Larry Craig and Mike Crapo (R–Idaho)
Judd Gregg and John Sununu (R–New Hampshire)
Same-state, different party Senators with most dissimilar voting records
Charles Grassley (R) and Tom Harkin (D) of Iowa
Pete Domenici (R) and Jeff Bingaman (D) of New Mexico
Wayne Allard (R) and Ken Salazar (D) of Colorado
Harry Reid (D) and John Ensign (R) of Nevada
Same-state, same party Senators with most dissimilar voting records
John McCain and Jon Kyl (R–Arizona)
Richard Shelby and Jeff Sessions (R–Alabama)
Kay Bailey Hutchison and John Cornyn (R–Texas)
Lindsey Graham and Jim DeMint (R–South Carolina)

Source: *National Journal*, 3 March 2007, pp. 36–37

Women in the 110th Congress

Congress in general, and the Senate in particular, has for most of its history been seen as a men's club. It was not until the passage of the 19th Amendment in 1920 that American women were guaranteed the vote in elections for

Congress. The first woman to serve in the Senate was 87-year-old Rebecca Felton, a Democrat from Georgia. She was appointed in 1922 but served only 1 day! Altogether, 35 women have served in the Senate. Two new women Senators were elected in 2006: Amy Klobuchar of Minnesota and Claire McCaskill of Missouri, both Democrats. That brings the number of women in the Senate to a record high of 16.

Three states — California, Maine and Washington — are currently represented in the Senate by two women: Barbara Boxer and Dianne Feinstein, both Democrats, represent California; Susan Collins and Olympia Snowe, both Republicans, represent Maine; and Patty Murray and Maria Cantwell, both Democrats, represent Washington state. As recently as the 96th Congress (1979–80), there was only one woman in Senate and even 10 years later, the 101st Congress (1989–90) included only two woman Senators.

With most female Senators being Democrats, the fact that the Democrats have regained control of the Senate means that women Senators have a higher profile in the 110th Congress, as well as greater numbers. Barbara Boxer of California chairs the Senate Environment and Public Works Committee, while her fellow Californian Dianne Feinstein chairs the Senate Rules and Administration Committee. And Senator Hillary Clinton of New York is widely regarded as the front-runner for the Democratic Party's presidential nomination in 2008.

In the House of Representatives, the 110th Congress has 71 (16%) women members, six more than at the start of the previous Congress. But here, again, the story for women is not just their increased numbers but their increased power. At the start of the 110th Congress, Nancy Pelosi (Democrat–California) was elected as the first woman House Speaker. The prestigious House Rules Committee also got its first woman chair, Louise Slaughter of New York.

Minorities in the 110th Congress

The 2006 mid-term elections brought the first black member to the US Senate since the defeat of Illinois Democrat Carol Moseley-Braun in 1998. Fellow Democrat Barack Obama was elected to the same seat, making him only the third popularly elected black Senator ever. Obama had made a well-received speech at the 2004 Democratic National Party Convention and at the time of writing is one of the front-runner candidates for the Democrats' 2008 presidential nomination. The number of Hispanics in the Senate remains at three, with the election to a full term of New Jersey Democrat Bob Menendez.

In the House, the number of black members remains constant at 41. But with the Democrats' takeover of the House, black people will have a far higher profile in the 110th Congress than they have had during their 12 years in the minority. James Clyburn was first elected to the House in 1992, a beneficiary of the 'majority–minority district' plans used in South Carolina, as well as in other mainly southern states. Clyburn was the first black representative from

South Carolina in more than a century. Now he is House Majority Whip — effectively number three in the Democratic leadership.

By virtue of their seniority, five other African-Americans became chairs of House standing committees at the start of the 110th Congress: Charles Rangel of New York (Ways and Means), John Conyers of Michigan (Judiciary), Bennie Thompson of Mississippi (Homeland Security), Stephanie Tubbs Jones of Ohio (Ethics) and Juanita Millender-McDonald of California (House Administration). However, Juanita Millender-McDonald died just months into the new Congress.

One significant loss for black representation in 2006 came in an open seat in Tennessee, where black Congressman Harold Ford sought election to the Senate — unsuccessfully in the event. Ford's district, centred on the city of Memphis, is three-fifths black and had been represented by a black member for over 30 years. But the Democratic primary was won by Steve Cohen, a white veteran state senator, and it is he who was elected to represent Ford's old district. The majority of black people in the House — 23 of the 41 — represent districts in which African-Americans are the racial majority.

The number of Hispanic members in the House remained unchanged from the start of the previous Congress, at 23. The House seat vacated by Bob Menendez in New Jersey was filled by another Hispanic Democrat, Albio Sires. Hispanics have made up a larger percentage of the US population since 2001 (14%) and there are now 24 majority-Hispanic House districts across the country. Yet Hispanics remain less well represented in the House. The reasons for this lie in the fact that Hispanic people have much lower levels of citizenship, voter registration and election participation than their black counterparts.

Other noteworthy minority arrivals at the 110th Congress were the first Buddhists to be elected to Congress: Mazie Hirono of Hawaii and Hank Johnson of Georgia. Hirono is Asian-American and Johnson is black, and both are Democrats. At the same time, Minnesota Democrat Keith Ellison was elected as the first Muslim member of Congress. The 110th Congress also saw an increase of Jewish members: 30 in the House (up from 26 in 2005) and 13 in the Senate (up from 11 in the previous Congress).

Age in the 110th Congress

The average age of Senators in the new Congress is just under 62, which breaks the record high set in the previous Congress by about 18 months. The average age of House members is 56, a year older than in the 109th Congress. The main reason for this significant increase in age is the low level of turnover in both chambers. The new Congress brought only 55 new House members (13% of the House) and 10 new Senators. The average length of service in the Senate is now 13 years — the longest in more than a century and therefore the longest since the Senate has been a directly elected chamber.

The 110th Congress includes four of the eight longest-serving Senators in the chamber's history. Robert Byrd (Democrat–West Virginia) is both the oldest and the longest serving. Senator Byrd was elected to a record-breaking ninth term in 2006, just 2 weeks before his 89th birthday. The others in the top four are Democrats Edward Kennedy of Massachusetts and Daniel Inouye of Hawaii, both first elected in 1962, and Republican Ted Stevens of Alaska, who has served since 1968.

Another reason for the increase in the average ages of Senators is that new members tend to be older when they are first elected. Just three of the ten new Senators are over a decade younger than their predecessors. Bernie Sanders, newly elected from Vermont, was 65 at the time of his election. In the House, the oldest member is Texas Republican Ralph Hall at 84. Eighty House members are older than 65.

Committees in the 110th Congress

Seniority rule

A rule stating that the chair of a congressional standing committee will be the member of the majority party with the longest continuous service on that committee.

In putting together their panel of standing committee chairs, the Democrats have deferred almost completely to the **seniority rule**. In all of the House standing committees bar one, the ranking minority member of the committee in the 109th Congress became the chair of the committee at the start of the 110th Congress. The one exception was at the Veterans' Affairs Committee, where Illinois Democrat Lane Evans had retired. But in his place the next in seniority, Bob Filner of California, took over the chair.

The Democrats have renamed a few of the House standing committees (see Table 2.3). The most significant change of title is the renaming of the House Government Reform Committee to the House *Oversight* and Government Reform Committee, a clear indication that the incoming Democrat majority wants to restore what they see as a lost — or at least little utilised — power of Congress.

Table 2.3 Titles of House standing committees in the 109th and 110th Congresses

House committee title in 109th Congress	House committee title in 110th Congress
Education and the Workforce	Education and Labor
Government Reform	Oversight and Government Reform
International Relations	Foreign Affairs
Resources	Natural Resources
Science	Science and Technology

It was the same story in the Senate, where in all but three standing committees the former ranking minority member took over the chair of the committee. At the Senate Banking Committee, the former ranking minority member, Paul Sarbanes of Maryland, retired at the end of the 109th Congress. His number two on the committee, Christopher Dodd of Connecticut, took over as chair. At the Environment Committee and at the Rules and Administration Committee, the top three Democrats by seniority opted to chair other committees, thus opening up the way for the fourth-ranking member to take over the chair of the committee — respectively Barbara Boxer and Dianne Feinstein, both of California.

Congressional Quarterly's weekly journal (16 April 2007) reported some interesting statistics on congressional committees in the new Congress. There are:

- **15** freshmen on the House Agriculture Committee, or one-third of the committee's membership. No other committee in the 110th Congress has more first-termers.
- **75** members of the House Transportation and Infrastructure Committee, making it the largest committee in Congress. The largest Senate committee — Appropriations — has 29 members.
- **7** members on the Senate Ethics Committee, making it the smallest congressional committee. The smallest in the House is House Administration, with nine members.
- **16** subcommittees in the House and Senate with the word 'oversight' in their name.
- **22** House committees or subcommittees chaired by Californians, more than any other state. New Yorkers chair 12, Massachusetts' House members nine and Texans eight.
- **2** senators from the same state serving on the following Senate committees: Agriculture (Iowa and Minnesota); Armed Services (Florida and Virginia); and Energy and Natural Resources (Oregon and New Mexico). This shows the special interest of those policy areas within the particular states.

In the same source, Rebecca Kimitch wrote of the importance of standing committees, both to Congress as a whole and to individual lawmakers:

> Committees, and most importantly their chairmen, stand as the gatekeepers to the House and Senate floor. Of the thousands of bills proposed every session, only a fraction make it to a committee mark-up — where they are shaped, refined and sometimes made palatable through amendments to factions in both parties.

> For individual lawmakers, committees are often where they carve out their niches of influence and expertise. Especially in the House, which committees lawmakers are assigned to, and whether they ever claim a leadership role, can make all the difference in their long-term success and satisfaction.

Members use their committee posts to wield power, bolster their re-election prospects (and fill their campaign treasuries) close to home. Republican Jerry Moran, who represents the vast grain-growing plains of western Kansas, has become an expert on farm economics on the Agriculture Committee. Democrat Luis Gutierrez, who represents largely immigrant Hispanic neighborhoods in Chicago, has become an expert in immigration policy in the Judiciary Committee.

All this is in stark contrast to the committees in the UK parliament, more a retirement home for failed ministers, has-beens, might-have-beens or thought-they-ought-to-have-beens, with little in the way of real political clout. Few self-respecting MPs would see a committee room as a place to carve out a 'niche of influence and expertise'. Indeed, one thing the British Conservative Party has been talking about is the revamping of UK parliamentary committees, to bring them more into line with their US counterparts. Whether that is possible in a parliamentary system is, perhaps, open to debate.

Questions

1 What is the current party balance in the Senate and the House of Representatives?
2 Explain how there is a regional basis of political ideology in US politics.
3 Explain in your own words the information presented in Table 2.2.
4 What does this chapter tell you about the trends regarding women in Congress?
5 Why are members of Congress who belong to racial minorities more influential in the 110th Congress than in previous years? Give some examples of minority members in leadership positions.
6 Explain in your own words the trends regarding age in Congress.
7 To what extent did the Democrats follow the seniority rule in deciding committee chairs at the start of the 110th Congress?
8 Why does Rebecca Kimitch think that standing committees are so important?

Dick Cheney: the most powerful vice-president?

What you need to know

- The vice-president is usually elected on a 'joint ticket' with the president.
- He (or doubtless some day she) becomes president on the death or resignation of the president.
- His few constitutional powers include acting as presiding officer of the Senate, where he has a casting vote in the case of a tie.
- Subsequent to the 25th Amendment, the vice-presidential office is now always occupied.
- The president may appoint a new vice-president if the office becomes vacant.
- The vice-president may become acting president if the president declares himself, or is declared, disabled.
- Traditionally, the office of vice-president was seen as something of a joke, though recently it has been regarded as more significant.

All change for the modern vice-presidency

Dick Cheney is the 46th vice-president of the United States. Not all holders of the office have been as public or as powerful as Cheney. You may have heard of the first two vice-presidents — John Adams (1789–97) and Thomas Jefferson (1797–1801) — who became, respectively, the second and third presidents. But it is unlikely you will know much about, or have even heard of, Daniel Tompkins (1817–25), Hannibal Hamlin (1861–65), Schuyler Colfax (1869–73), or Alben Barkley (1949–53). Between 1801 and 1953, the office was generally filled by politicians whose names quickly passed into the mists of political anonymity.

The situation began to change when Richard Nixon became vice-president in 1953. Of the 11 vice-presidents from Nixon to Cheney, four became president and three others were subsequently nominated as the presidential candidate of their party (see Table 3.1). With a number of modern-day presidents coming to the Oval Office without any experience in Congress, the modern vice-president — often someone who has served in Congress — has played a key role in liaison between the White House and Capitol Hill.

Table 3.1 Vice-presidents 1953–present, showing later political career

Vice-president	Years in office	Later political career
Richard Nixon (R)	1953–61	President (1969–74)
Lyndon Johnson (D)	1961–63	President (1963–69)
Hubert Humphrey (D)	1965–69	Presidential candidate (1968)
Spiro Agnew (R)	1969–73	Resigned
Gerald Ford (R)	1973–74	President (1974–77)
Nelson Rockefeller (R)	1974–77	—
Walter Mondale (D)	1977–81	Presidential candidate (1984)
George H. W. Bush (R)	1981–89	President (1989–93)
Dan Quayle (R)	1989–93	—
Al Gore (D)	1993–2001	Presidential candidate (2000)
Dick Cheney (R)	2001–	—

Nine of the 11 most recent vice-presidents served in Congress. The only two not to have done so were Spiro Agnew and Nelson Rockefeller, both of whom had served as state governors. Vice-Presidents Mondale, Bush, Gore and Cheney all served as number two to presidents who had no previous Washington experience, and their periods in office cover 28 of the 32 years between 1977 and 2009. Indeed, 33 of the 46 vice-presidents (72%) have previously served in Congress.

The modern vice-presidency is different not only in the kind of person who fills the office but also in the fact that the office is always filled. Until 1967, the office was frequently empty — for around 37 of the 176 years (21%) between 1789 and 1965. This was because for the first 18 decades or so of the US constitutional system, there was no mechanism for filling the office of the vice-president when the incumbent either ascended to the presidency (which occurred eight times), died (which occurred seven times) or resigned (once). And an office that was empty for almost a quarter of the time was hardly going to be regarded as one of high esteem and power.

When it came to choosing the vice-presidential candidate, the conventional wisdom was that the number two slot would go to someone who would 'balance the ticket' — in other words, someone who would appeal to groups of voters to whom the presidential candidate would not appeal. For this reason John F. Kennedy — a young, liberal, northeastern Catholic — chose Lyndon Johnson — a much older, more conservative, southern protestant — as his vice-presidential candidate in 1960. Choosing the vice-president was all about votes rather than governing. Not so in the summer of 2000, when Republican presidential candidate Governor George W. Bush chose Dick Cheney as his vice-presidential running-mate.

From Wyoming to the White House

When Dick Cheney became vice-president in January 2001, he was probably more qualified for the role than any of his 45 predecessors. He had already been in and around Washington politics — at both ends of Pennsylvania Avenue — for over 30 years. The 27-year-old Cheney had arrived in Washington back in 1968 as a Capitol Hill staff member. From there he progressed to the Nixon White House and then to that of Gerald Ford. By 1975, he was White House Chief of Staff — at 34, the youngest person ever to hold the post.

These years in the Nixon–Ford administration were formative to Cheney's views of how Washington works. For it was during this period that Cheney became convinced that presidential power, far from being a threat in itself, was significantly under threat by a resurgent and power-grabbing Congress. This thesis of presidential power would come to dominate his post-9/11 view of Washington politics.

Cheney left the White House in January 1977 and the following year was elected to the House of Representatives to represent Wyoming. Within a decade he rose to become House Minority Whip, the number two leadership post in the House Republican caucus. In 1989, he was appointed as Secretary of Defense by the first President Bush, a post he held for 4 years.

Cheney had seemingly retired from politics by 1993 and he spent 7 years as chief executive of Halliburton, an oil services firm. In 2000, Governor George W. Bush put Cheney in charge of the search team for his vice-presidential candidate. Bush quickly became convinced that the man in charge of the search was the man he wanted in the post.

Coming from rock-solid Republican Wyoming, with its three Electoral College votes, Bush clearly did not pick Cheney for his electoral appeal. He chose him because he brought experience and gravitas to a potential Bush presidency. Thus Cheney arrived as vice-president in January 2001 as a former White House Chief of Staff, senior member of Congress and Secretary of Defense. It was an unprecedented CV for someone in what used to be a much-reviled and despised office: the vice-presidency of the United States.

'I have a different understanding with the President'

Back in 1980, when Governor Ronald Reagan was looking for a suitable vice-presidential candidate, Reagan's advisers hit on the idea of trying to recruit former President Ford as Reagan's number two. It was an ingenious plan, one that was described by many commentators as the 'dream ticket'. The former president was approached, but said he would accept only if he were to be given some specific and meaningful role — a kind of co-presidency. Accounts at the time suggested that Ford was being advised by his former Secretary of State Henry Kissinger. But at a conference in 2000 of former White House

Chiefs of Staff, Cheney disclosed that he had been deeply involved. Ford 'made a number of requests in terms of his influence over the budget, personnel, foreign policy etc.', Cheney recalled. In the end, both Reagan and Ford drew back on the deal, fearing a splintering of presidential power.

Ford's shopping list looks uncannily like a job description of the Cheney vice-presidency. For by the time Cheney arrived in the vice-president's office in 2001, he had 'put a great deal of thought into how a vice president can transform himself from a funeral-trotting figurehead into a centre of real power' (*Washington Post*, 'A Strong Push from Backstage', 26 June 2007).

In the early days of the Bush administration, Washington insiders joked about the contrast between the President's inexperience and the Vice-President's prodigious CV. 'Just think', someone once quipped, 'if Dick Cheney were assassinated, Bush would have to become president!' Hidden within the joke was a recognition of the significance that Dick Cheney had already achieved in the role.

Someone who met Vice-President Dick Cheney during his first few weeks in office was former Vice-President Dan Quayle (1989–93). As Quayle remembers, he dropped in to see the new vice-president in the White House in January 2001. Quayle told Cheney: 'Dick, you know, you're going to be doing a lot of this international travelling, you're going to be doing all this political fundraising, you'll be going to the funerals, I mean, this is what vice-presidents do. We've all done it.' Quayle remembers that Cheney 'got that little smile and replied: "I have a different understanding with the President."' Quayle commented: '[Cheney] had the understanding with President Bush that he would be "surrogate chief of staff".'

Joshua Bolten, who has served as Chief of Staff during Bush's second term, recalls what happened as the Bush team was preparing for office back in 2000–01. 'I remember at the outset, during the transition, thinking "What do vice presidents do?"' Bolten said that the traditional model was to give the vice-president a particular field of interest to look after. For Dan Quayle it was the Council on Competitiveness, and for Al Gore the National Partnership for Reinventing Government. Bolten recalls that Cheney 'did not particularly warm to that'. Cheney preferred, and Bush approved, a mandate that gave him access to 'every table and every meeting', making his voice heard in 'whatever area the vice president feels he wants to be active in'.

Mary Matalin, who was Counsellor to the Vice-President for the first 2 years of the administration, describes Cheney's portfolio as 'the iron issues' — a list that comprised the core concerns of every recent president. According to Matalin, Cheney would take on 'the economic issues, the security issues, the energy issues and the White House legislative agenda thereby becoming the go-to guy on Capitol Hill'. Other close aides recall how much influence Cheney had in nominations and appointments.

Such policy inputs are unprecedented and a far cry from the conventional view of the vice-presidency, about which more put-down quips and jokes have been made than any other office in US politics.

The man in the bunker on 9/11

On 11 September 2001, the President, the White House Chief of Staff and many others of the presidential entourage were in Sarasota, Florida, 1,500 km south of Washington DC. The Chairman of the Joint Chiefs, General Henry Shelton, was on a plane heading east across the Atlantic bound for Europe. The Secretary of State, Colin Powell, was in Lima, Peru. Dick Cheney was in his West Wing office at the White House.

At just after 9.30 a.m., Secret Service agents burst into his office and told Cheney, 'Sir, we have to leave immediately.' Without waiting for a vice-presidential response, the agents grabbed Cheney under his arms, virtually lifting him off the ground as they propelled him into the secure bunker — officially known as the Presidential Emergency Operations Center (PEOC) — below the East Wing of the White House. Cheney was joined in the PEOC by other top administration officials and staffers, including National Security Adviser Condoleezza Rice and Transportation Secretary Norman Mineta. A few minutes later a plane hit the Pentagon, the home of the Department of Defense, just a couple of miles from the White House.

Having learnt that the Pentagon had been hit, Cheney telephoned the President, who was en route to Sarasota Airport, and told him not to return to Washington 'until we can find out what the hell is going on'. Once Bush was on board Air Force One, Cheney phoned the President again, recommending that the President authorise the military to shoot down any plane under the control of hijackers. Unaware that Flight 93 had already crashed in Pennsylvania, the Secret Service asked Cheney for permission to shoot it down. There is some disagreement as to whether Cheney authorised the shooting down of Flight 93 or whether he checked first with the President. As by this time the plane had already crashed, the discussion is moot.

What there is little disagreement about is that the Vice-President was the chief enforcer in keeping the President away from Washington for most of that fateful day. When Air Force One made its first landing, at Barksdale Air Force Base, there was an argument between Bush and Cheney as to where the President should go to next. Cheney insisted throughout the day that there was a 'credible terrorist threat' to Air Force One that prevented the President's return to Washington. Others believe this was a Cheney invention. Whatever the truth, it is clear that Cheney's impact on the events of 9/11 was critical. It was also highly significant that when President Bush gave evidence to the September 11 Commission, he insisted on having Cheney with him.

Planning for the 'war on terror'

Before the end of the day on 11 September, it was the Vice-President who began asking the question: 'what extraordinary powers will the President need for his response to the events of 9/11?' According to *Washington Post* reporters Barton Gellman and Jo Becker:

> More than any one man in the months to come, Cheney freed Bush to fight the 'war on terror' as he saw it, animated by their shared belief that al-Qaeda's destruction would require what the Vice-President called 'robust interrogation' to extract intelligence from captured suspects. With a small coterie of allies, Cheney supplied the rationale and the political muscle to drive far-reaching legal changes through the White House, the Justice Department and the Pentagon.

It was the Vice-President who was behind the broad wording of the authorisation of action approved by Congress on 18 September. And it was from this authorisation that Cheney recommended the interception of communications to and from the United States without a warrant, which had been forbidden by federal law since 1978. It was an extraordinary bypassing of both Congress and the courts.

When, on 25 October 2001, the chairs and ranking minority members of the congressional intelligence committees were summoned for a secret briefing at the White House on the eavesdropping programme, they were taken not to the Oval Office, but to the Vice-President's office. The President told Senator Bob Graham (Republican–Florida, the then chairman of the Senate Intelligence Committee): 'The vice-president is your point of contact in the White House. He has the portfolio for intelligence activities.'

It was the Vice-President and his allies who, according to more than two dozen current and former Bush administration officials, pioneered the distinction between forbidden 'torture' and the permitted use of 'cruel, inhuman or degrading' methods of questioning terrorist suspects. After the revelations of the abuse at the Abu Ghraib prison in Iraq in 2004, this policy too received significant rebuffs from both Congress and the courts. On 5 October 2005, the Republican-controlled Senate voted 90–9 in favour of Senator John McCain's Detainee Treatment Act, which included the language of the Geneva Convention concerning torture. It was, by any measure, a rebuke to the Vice-President. Bush signed the bill into law. 'Well, I don't win all the arguments', Cheney told the *Wall Street Journal* at the time.

It was Cheney who put in place the military commissions to conduct the questioning of terrorist suspects held at Guantanamo Bay. It was Cheney who first voiced in public (at a US Chamber of Commerce conference on 14 November 2001) that terrorists do not 'deserve to be treated as prisoners of war', long before the President had made any such decision. Within a few years, the courts would rule otherwise.

On 29 June 2006, the Supreme Court struck its sharpest blow to the powers that the Vice-President had asserted when it ruled in the case of *Hamdan* v *Rumsfeld,* by five votes to three, that the President had no lawful power to try alleged terrorists in military commissions. The White House then had to spend the autumn of 2006 negotiating with Congress on the Military Commissions Act that would pass muster with the Supreme Court. Chief of Staff Joshua Bolten admitted that the legislation that Bush eventually signed 'did not come out exactly as the Vice-President would have wanted'.

But through all this, the power of the vice-presidency has been extraordinarily significant. It has at times seemed almost like a co-presidency. Yet Cheney would probably not see it this way — for him, protecting the power of the *president* is what is most important.

Cheney's views on presidential power

Back in November 1980, just weeks before the Reagan administration took up residency in Washington, James Baker — who was about to assume the role of White House Chief of Staff — went to Capitol Hill for a meeting with Republican congressman Dick Cheney. Remember that Cheney had served as Chief of Staff in the Ford administration just 4 years earlier. The advice that Cheney gave to Baker on that November day is revealing about Cheney's views on presidential power. We know much of what Cheney said, because Baker's notes of the meeting have been released recently (see Box 3.1).

Box 3.1 Extracts from notes made by James Baker (White House Chief of Staff designate) of conversation with Dick Cheney, 19 November 1980

Cheney: 11/19/80
- Defense and Treasury Secretaries really too busy.
- Chief of Staff: make all trips with President.
- Presidency seriously weakened in recent years.
- Restore power and authority to executive branch. Need strong leadership. Get rid of War Powers Act.
- Strong Cabinet and strong staff in White House. Not 'either or' proposition. Have to have both.
- Orderly schedule and orderly paper flow is way to protect the President. Well designed system. Got to be brutal in scheduling decisions. Need to have discipline and order and be discriminating.
- Stay away from 'oh by the way' decisions. Can hurt the President. Bring it up at Cabinet meeting. Make sure everyone understands this.
- Requests from Cabinet members to see President — [they] have to [see him].
- BE AN HONEST BROKER.
- Keep a low profile.
- Press Secretary — not a press guy in Oval Office but a President's guy in press room.

Source: **www.washingtonpost.com**

US Government & Politics

It would be true to say that Dick Cheney had left the White House in January 1977 at what was the low point of presidential power. Nixon had been forced to resign. Ford had no national mandate, not even as vice-president (he was appointed by Nixon). Congress was trying to regain what it perceived as its lost power. There was the Church Committee investigating the CIA, the passage of the War Powers Act, the Budget and Impoundment Control Act and the Case Act. Congress frequently overrode Ford's vetoes. All this was bad news to the young Dick Cheney.

Despite his later membership of that august body, Cheney saw Congress as weak and indecisive, unsuited to making well-informed, speedy decisions — especially those in the area of defence and national security policy. In 1983, Cheney — by then a House member from Wyoming — told an American Enterprise Institute conference that Congress was 'all too often swayed by the public opinion of the moment' and was incapable of making the swift decisions required in 'a dangerous and hostile world'. In a turn of phrase he used many times post-9/11, but originally spoken in the context of President Reagan's invasion of Grenada, Cheney claimed that it 'might have cost hundreds of lives' if Reagan had waited for 'the usual dialogue and debate about whether Congress would authorise action'.

Cheney continued back then:

> Simply by creating a defence establishment, Congress has already given prior approval for any presidential decision on where and how to make war. We have appropriated the funds and raised the army and purchased the equipment and built the missiles and the bombers, and the president has the authority to make decisions about how to use those things.

Four years later, in 1987, Congressman Dick Cheney issued a blistering attack on the report by a congressional select committee on the so-called Iran-Contra Affair. According to Cheney, the scandal was not that the White House had broken the law, but that Congress had tried to command the commander-in-chief. Reagan's decisions, according to Cheney, may not always have been wise, but they were 'constitutionally protected exercises of inherent presidential powers'. According to David Gergen, who worked with Cheney during the Ford years, Cheney 'felt that what had become known as the imperial presidency during the Nixon years had become the imperilled presidency'. But while others thought that the balance had been readjusted during the 1980s and 1990s, when Dick Cheney arrived in Washington in 2001 he thought that the job of reasserting presidential power was still very much 'work in progress'.

Some who have known Cheney over many years ask where is the mainstream conservative they once knew? What these extracts show is that Cheney's views on presidential power have remained remarkably constant. What has changed is his power to promote them.

Influence on domestic policy

It would be wrong to think that Vice-President Cheney has been influential only on matters of foreign, defence and national security policy. Far from it. In 2003, it was Cheney who was the President's chief salesman on Capitol Hill for his centrepiece tax cut plan. When the space shuttle *Columbia* disintegrated in Texas on 1 February 2003, President Bush was consumed with concern for the families of the dead astronauts and adopted the role of comforter-in-chief. He left the Vice-President to make the critical decisions about the future of manned space flights.

The Vice-President chairs a budget review board, a panel the Bush administration created to set spending priorities and serve as arbiter when cabinet members appeal against the decisions made by the Office of Management and Budget.

It was Dick Cheney's insistence on easing air pollution controls, not the personal reasons she cited at the time, which led Christine Todd Whitman to resign as the administrator of the Environmental Protection Agency in June 2003. It was also Cheney who pushed to make Nevada's Yucca Mountain a repository for nuclear waste — another victory of industry over environment during this administration.

In May 2005, a small group met to discuss who might succeed the ailing Chief Justice of the United States, William Rehnquist. As Jo Becker and Barton Gellman later recounted in the *Washington Post*:

> The meeting wasn't held at the White House or the Justice Department. And the highest-ranking official in the room wasn't the Attorney General or the White House Chief of Staff, the White House Counsel or the President's chief political adviser, although they were all there. It was Vice President Dick Cheney, and it was to an unpretentious room off the Vice President's quarters that potential candidates were summoned for interviews.

The candidates who got through the initial interviews led by the Vice-President's selection committee would then go on to a more 'relaxed' interview with the President. It was Cheney who asked about candidates' judicial philosophies and case histories; the President was more interested in personal matters. Cheney's group started with 11 potential nominees but ended with a shortlist of five.

On 19 July 2005, the President drew from the Cheney-vetted five when he nominated John Roberts to replace the retiring Sandra Day O'Connor. It was the Vice-President's office that took the lead in introducing Roberts, both on Capitol Hill and to the national media. Then in September, Chief Justice Rehnquist died. The President moved Roberts to the post of Chief Justice, leaving the O'Connor vacancy still unfilled. The President now ignored the Vice-President's list. First he floated the idea of nominating Alberto Gonzales to the Supreme Court. Gonzales was not one of Cheney's five. When that idea ran out of steam, Chief of Staff Andrew Card was sent to tell the Vice-President that White House Counsel Harriet Miers was to be nominated. She was not one of the five either. Cheney was not amused. 'Didn't have the nerve to tell me himself', Cheney was reported to have commented in a rare show of disloyalty. In public, Cheney defended the nomination. When Miers withdrew, Bush nominated Samuel Alito, another of Cheney's recommended five. 'That Cheney should play such an unprecedented role in vetting potential [Supreme Court] candidates is a measure of the trust Bush places in him' wrote David Yalof, the author of a noted book on Supreme Court nominations (*Pursuit of Justices: Presidential Politics and the Selection of Supreme Court Nominees*, 2001).

Cheney's legacy

According to a *New York Times* editorial entitled 'Mr Cheney's Imperial Presidency' (23 December 2005):

> George W. Bush has quipped several times during his political career that it would be much easier to govern in a dictatorship. Apparently he never told his vice president that this was a joke. Virtually from the time he chose himself to be Mr Bush's running mate in 2000, Dick Cheney has spearheaded an extraordinary expansion of the powers of the presidency — from writing energy policy behind closed doors with oil executives to abrogating long-standing treaties and using the 9/11 attacks as a pretext to invade Iraq, scrap the Geneva Convention and spy on American citizens.

Dick Cheney has certainly fought tenaciously for increased presidential power. His efforts have received setbacks at the hands of both Congress and the courts. Cheney has, as we have seen, been hugely powerful as vice-president, more powerful than any of his 45 predecessors. David Nather wrote in *Congressional Quarterly Weekly* (11 June 2007):

> Cheney's impact on the Bush presidency — his role in the build up to the Iraq War, his influence on anti-terrorism policies such as eavesdropping and interrogation tactics, and his expansive view of executive power — has been so widespread that his status as the most powerful vice president in history isn't seriously debated any more.

But will the Cheney vice-presidency change the office in the long term? Possibly not, for three reasons.

First, because he is probably the first vice-president since Alben Barkley (1949–53) to have no presidential ambitions of his own, this has put Cheney in an unusually strong position. The President felt entirely unthreatened by his powerful vice-president. This would be unlikely to be the case in most future administrations.

Second, there has been a huge mismatch between the political experience of the President and that of the Vice-President. George W. Bush had a political

CV that resembled more that of an old-style vice-president, while Dick Cheney looked more qualified for high office than most recent presidents.

Third, the events of 9/11 and those that followed gave Dick Cheney a peculiar environment in which to operate. 'All the stars aligned correctly for Cheney,' commented Republican House member Ray LaHood of Illinois. 'He probably had more experience than any vice-president in history and he was part of an administration that had little or no experience governing.' Cheney took the combination of factors and has played it for all its worth. Successors probably will not have the same opportunities.

That is not to suggest that the vice-presidency post-Cheney will revert to pre-Nixon obscurity. Cheney is not the first modern vice-president to be regarded as significant and influential.

> It's only 2 o'clock in the afternoon, but the Vice President has already been in the Oval Office three times for private chats with his boss. Here is a vice president not only exercising power but revelling in it, surrounded by scurrying aides and history in the making.

Dick Cheney? No. This is an extract from *Time* magazine in May 1977, talking about the role of Vice-President Walter Mondale in the Carter White House.

One consequence we may see as a result of Dick Cheney's unparalleled influence is a much closer vetting of the vice-presidential nominees that the Democratic and Republican Party presidential candidates choose in 2008. 'The vice-president's importance will probably be raised in many, many years, because of the Cheney phenomenon,' commented constitutional lawyer Bruce Fein. Questions may well be asked of future nominees, not only as to whether they are qualified enough to succeed to the Oval Office, but whether they are qualified enough to succeed to Dick Cheney's office.

The challenge for Congress — and, to some extent, for the public — will be to decide whether any corrective measures are needed when a vice-president exerts so much influence in an administration and uses it in such controversial and significant ways. Congress is not entirely helpless in this situation. It does have its executive oversight powers. Congress also votes the money for the vice-president's staff, so it could use the power of the purse to limit the size of the office. But, like the president, the vice-president is immune from testifying before congressional committees. 'We can't get [the vice-president] in front of us,' said Senator Carl Levin (Democrat–Michigan), chair of the investigation subcommittee of the Senate's Homeland Security and Governmental Affairs Committee.

The most likely restraint on the power of future vice-presidents will not be Congress but the president. It is difficult to imagine a President Hillary Clinton, or whoever, being willing to allow their vice-president the kind of unbridled power enjoyed by Dick Cheney. Future presidents would be wise, however, to define the boundaries of vice-presidential power rather carefully.

Questions

1 In what ways has the office of the vice-presidency changed since the 1950s with regard to the kind of people who become vice-president?
2 Explain the term 'balance the ticket' with regard to how the vice-presidential candidate is typically chosen.
3 Write a paragraph detailing Dick Cheney's political career before he became vice-president in 2001.
4 Explain what Dick Cheney meant by saying: 'I have a different understanding with the President.'
5 Explain Dick Cheney's role on 11 September 2001.
6 Describe the various ways in which Dick Cheney played a central role in foreign policy-making and relations with Congress in the period after 9/11.
7 Explain Cheney's views concerning presidential and congressional power.
8 Describe the extent to which Cheney has influenced domestic policy under George W. Bush.
9 Why does the chapter conclude that the Cheney vice-presidency will possibly not change the vice-presidency in the long term?

Information for this chapter was drawn from a series of articles in the *Washington Post* (24–27 June 2007) and an article in *Congressional Quarterly Weekly*, 'A Power Surge Under Scrutiny' (11 June 2007).

Chapter 4

The Supreme Court, 2006–07

What you need to know

- The Supreme Court is the highest federal court in the USA.
- Supreme Court justices are appointed by the president and confirmed by the Senate.
- They are appointed for life.
- There are nine justices on the Supreme Court: one chief justice and eight associate justices.
- Of the current nine justices, seven have been appointed by Republican presidents and only two by Democrats.
- The Supreme Court has the power of judicial review. This is the power to declare acts of Congress or actions of the executive branch — or acts or actions of state governments — unconstitutional, and thereby null and void.
- By this power of judicial review, the Court acts as the umpire of the Constitution and plays a leading role in safeguarding Americans' rights and liberties.

The 2006–07 session of the Supreme Court was noteworthy for being the first full term in which both Chief Justice John Roberts (appointed 2005) and Samuel Alito (appointed 2006) served throughout. Court watchers therefore wanted to see to what extent their replacing, respectively, of Chief Justice Rehnquist and Associate Justice O'Connor affected the judgements handed down by the Court.

Table 4.1 Significant Supreme Court decisions, 2006–07 term

Case	Concerning	Decision
Gonzales v Carhart	Ban on late-term abortions upheld	5–4
Parents Involved v Seattle	School desegregation	5–4
FEC v Wisconsin Right to Life	Curbs on pre-election television advertisements weakened	5–4
Morse v Frederick	Freedom of speech	5–4
Hein v Freedom from Religion Foundation	Faith-based organisations	5–4
Panetti v Quarterman	Execution of schizophrenics	5–4

The session will also be remembered for the Court handing down two landmark decisions — one on abortion, another on the issue of race in school admissions. In these decisions, the Court was to some extent revisiting two great decisions of the twentieth century — *Roe* v *Wade* (1973) on abortion and *Brown* v *Board of Education of Topeka* (1954) on the link between race and schools' admissions policies. Table 4.1 shows the cases from the 2006–07 session that we will be considering in this chapter.

The 2006–07 term

Abortion rights

On Wednesday 18 April 2007, the Supreme Court handed down what will almost certainly go down as a landmark decision of the Roberts Court, upholding the Partial-Birth Abortion Ban Act. The 5–4 majority decision in the case of *Gonzales* v *Carhart* was written by Anthony Kennedy and was joined by the four conservative members of the Court: Chief Justice Roberts and Associate Justices Samuel Alito, Clarence Thomas and Antonin Scalia. Here was another instance of the Court chipping away at the right of a woman to an abortion, as declared by the Court back in 1973 in the case of *Roe* v *Wade*.

First, some background to this decision. Most abortions — probably well over 90% — are performed within the first 3 months of pregnancy. The procedure ends with the doctor vacuuming out the embryonic tissue. This procedure is unaffected by the recent decision. However, if the abortion occurs much later in the pregnancy then some form of surgical operation is required. The woman will be placed under anaesthetic, her cervix dilated and the foetus removed in pieces.

Some doctors use a different procedure for these 'late-term' abortions, to reduce risks to the woman of bleeding, infection and permanent injury. This other procedure involves partly delivering the foetus and then crushing its skull to make removal easier. Opponents say this amounts to infanticide, as the foetus could be viable (able to survive outside the uterus) at the time. It is this procedure that Congress voted to ban in the so-called Partial-Birth Abortion Ban Act in 2003.

The Republican-controlled Congress had passed the legislation twice before, in the 1990s. But on both occasions, Democrat President Bill Clinton vetoed the legislation — first in April 1996 and again in October 1997. Both times Clinton's veto was sustained in Congress. While the House of Representatives voted to override the President's veto (by 285 votes to 137 in 1996, and by 296 votes to 132 in 1997), the Senate failed on both occasions to override the veto, being nine votes short (57–41) in 1996 and just three votes short (64–36) in 1997 of the required two-thirds majority. However, with Republican George W. Bush elected in 2000 and Republicans still in control of both houses of Congress, the Partial-Birth Abortion Ban Act was passed by Congress and signed into law by the President in 2003.

Writing for the majority in upholding the legislation, Justice Kennedy announced that 'the government may use its voice and its regulatory authority to show respect for the life within the woman'. He continued: 'While we find no reliable data to measure the phenomenon, it seems unexceptional to conclude some women come to regret their choice to abort the infant life they once created and sustained'. For the minority, Justice Ruth Bader Ginsburg stated that the majority opinion of the Court in this case 'cannot be understood as anything other than an effort to chip away at a right declared again and again in this court — and with increasing comprehension of its centrality to women's lives'. Justice Ginsburg said that the majority opinion was too paternalistic in its attitude towards women. 'The solution the Court approves,' Ginsburg stated, 'is not to require doctors to inform women adequately of the different procedures they might choose and the risk each entails. Instead the Court shields women by denying them any choice in the matter.'

President Bush, in an immediate statement from the White House, said that the Court's decision 'affirms the Constitution, does not stand in the way of people's representatives enacting laws reflecting the compassion and humanity of America', adding that 'the Supreme Court's decision is an affirmation of the progress we have made over the past 6 years in protecting human dignity and upholding the sanctity of life'. In contrast, Democrat House Speaker Nancy Pelosi described the decision as 'a significant step backwards' for abortion rights of women.

This was a most significant decision for three reasons. First — and for the first time in its history — the Court declared that a specific abortion procedure could be banned and made no exception for the health of the woman, although it did provide an exception if the life of the woman was threatened. This decision was therefore seen by Democrats and liberal activist groups as a serious in-road into abortion rights as announced by the Court in 1973.

Second, the decision showed the significance of the change of membership of the Court with the switch of conservative Samuel Alito for the more moderate (especially on abortion rights) Sandra Day O'Connor, who had retired in 2006. Back in 2000, in *Stenberg* v *Carhart*, the Court had struck down a Nebraska state law prohibiting the same late-term procedure. This was another 5–4 decision, but on that occasion the liberal wing of the Court — Justices Souter, Ginsburg, Breyer and Stevens — had been joined by Sandra Day O'Connor. O'Connor, while recognising that the procedure used in such cases could be 'gruesome', nonetheless decided that it was sometimes necessary. In 2007, the Court upheld a federal law very similar to the Nebraska statute with Bush-appointee Samuel Alito swinging the case to the conservative majority. As Joan Biskupic wrote in her editorial comment in *USA Today* (18 April 2007): 'The Supreme Court's abortion ruling was a reminder of the Court's rightward turn since the addition of Bush appointee Samuel Alito.'

Third, the decision has potential political significance in terms of the party political debate on abortion, the possible outcomes of the presidential and congressional races scheduled for 2008, as well as for policy-making in various states. Conservative interest groups, such as Concerned Women for America, the Eagle Forum and the National Right to Life Committee were jubilant at the Court's decision. Such groups are now fired up to press for states to pass legislation further limiting abortion rights. Whereas such groups used to see their goal as getting the Court to overturn the *Roe* v *Wade* decision, now they take a much more incremental approach — the 'chipping away' of which Justice Ginsburg spoke in her dissenting opinion. One idea being pushed by pro-life groups is to persuade states to pass legislation that would mandate an ultrasound scan of the foetus as part of the abortion counselling process.

By bringing the abortion debate right back to the centre of the political arena just before a new round of presidential and congressional elections, the Supreme Court's decision has also fired up liberal, pro-choice groups. Groups such as the National Women's Political Caucus and Planned Parenthood say that the Court's ruling has rallied their members too, increasing fundraising revenue and putting new pressure on Democrat candidates (whether for the White House or Congress) to defend women's rights more vigorously. Leon Panetta, a former White House Chief of Staff to President Bill Clinton, had this to say in a *National Journal* interview (26 May 2007):

> I think there had been some sense that social issues would be on the back burner in [the 2008] election and the main focus would be more on the Iraq war, health care and the environment. But what [the Supreme Court] decision did was to essentially push the abortion issue back into one of the top issues that candidates are going to be asked about.

This only goes to show how far-reaching and significant Supreme Court decisions can be.

Racial balance in schools

The Court's other landmark decision of this term centred on a couple of cases relating to the use of race to determine which students should attend which schools, in an attempt to achieve racial balance in what Americans call 'public schools' — that is, state schools. In the two cases decided jointly by the Court — *Parents Involved in Community Schools Inc.* v *Seattle School District* and *Meredith* v *Jefferson County (Kentucky) Board of Education* — the Supreme Court declared it unconstitutional to assign students to public schools solely for the purpose of achieving racial balance. Both school systems centred upon racial quotas of white and minority representation in schools that would not otherwise be achieved because of racially segregated housing patterns in Seattle, Washington and Louisville, Kentucky.

For example, in Louisville, the student allocation programme was devised to ensure that the proportion of black students in the city's schools did not fall below 15% or exceed 50% in any school. The case was brought by the mother of a child who was denied a transfer to his chosen school because the school he wanted to leave needed to keep its white pupils in order to stay within the programme's racial quota. The Seattle case was brought by a group of parents who had formed a non-profit organisation to fight the city's race-based high school assignment programme.

Once again, the Court was split 5–4 and again it was the conservative coalition (Roberts, Scalia, Thomas and Alito, joined by Justice Kennedy) who formed the majority in this decision. Both sides saw themselves as protecting the equal protection rights announced in the 1954 landmark decision of *Brown* v *Board of Education of Topeka*. Writing for the majority, Chief Justice Roberts stated that:

> Before *Brown*, school children were told where they could and could not go to school based on the colour of their skin. The school districts in these cases have not carried the heavy burden of demonstrating that we should allow this once again — even for very different reasons. The way to stop discrimination on the basis of race is to stop discriminating on the basis of race.

The Chief Justice also made it clear that he and his conservative colleagues on the Court have a concern that allocating students to schools on the basis of racial quotas violates the equal protection clause of the Constitution's 14th Amendment. 'Simply because the school districts may seek a worthy goal does not mean they are free to discriminate on the basis of race to achieve it,' Roberts declared. Justice Clarence Thomas, the Court's only black member and a solid conservative, wrote waspishly that what the dissenting minority would really like to do would be to 'constitutionalise today's faddish social theories,' adding that 'if our history has taught us anything, it has taught us to beware of elites bearing racial theories'. Ouch!

Writing for the Court's liberal minority, Justice Stephen Breyer said the decision was one 'the Court and the nation will come to regret'. Also alluding to the 1954 ruling, Breyer continued:

> The lesson of history is not that efforts to continue racial segregation are constitutionally indistinguishable from efforts to achieve racial integration. Indeed, it is a cruel distortion of history to compare Topeka, Kansas, in the 1950s with Louisville and Seattle in the modern day.

But the decision was complicated by the fact that although Justice Anthony Kennedy cast the deciding vote in agreeing with the Court's conservatives to strike down the racial quota programmes, he refused to sign up to about half of the majority opinion and issued his own opinion as well. Kennedy stated:

> Parts of the opinion by the Chief Justice imply an all too unyielding insistence that race cannot be a factor in instances when, in my view, it may be taken into account. The plurality opinion is too dismissive of the

legitimate interest government has in ensuring all people have equal opportunities regardless of race.

Justice Kennedy said that in his opinion, some race-based solutions to school segregation would be acceptable: the redrawing of school attendance zones and strategic site selection of new schools, for example.

What effect this somewhat muddled decision will have on the public school systems across the United States is somewhat unclear. Some school districts have already altered their student allocation programmes because lower courts had already declared them unconstitutional. For example, in the vicinity of Washington DC, Montgomery County ceased to consider race in assigning children to schools in 2000 when the US Court of Appeals declared their race-based allocation policy to be unconstitutional.

Campaign finance

In the case of *Federal Election Commission* v *Wisconsin Right to Life*, the Court weakened curbs on pre-election television commercials, thereby striking down a key provision of the Bipartisan Campaign Reform Act (otherwise known as the McCain–Feingold Campaign Finance Reform Act) of 2002. The 2002 Act stated that business corporations and labour unions could no longer pay for television advertisements that mentioned candidates in presidential or congressional elections in the 30 days before a primary election or in the 60 days before a general election. The 2007 decision struck down that ban as unconstitutional as, in the view of the Court's majority, it violated the freedom of speech provisions of the 1st Amendment.

Extract from 1st Amendment (1791)

Congress shall make no law...abridging the freedom of speech.

Here was yet another 5–4 decision by the Court, and once more it was the Court's conservatives mentioned above who formed the majority. 'Discussion of issues cannot be suppressed simply because the issues may also be pertinent in an election', wrote Chief Justice Roberts in the majority opinion. 'Where the First Amendment is implicated, the tie goes to the speaker, not the censor.' For the minority, Justice David Souter believed the clock had been turned back to the bad old days of rampant campaign spending by corporate 'fat cats' and labour unions. 'After today,' wrote Justice Souter, 'the ban on contributions by corporations and unions and the limitation on their corrosive spending when they enter the political arena are open to easy circumvention, and the possibilities for regulating corporate and union campaign money are unclear.'

The case was noteworthy in uniting two usually opposing groups: the US Chamber of Commerce and the AFL-CIO (the American equivalent of the British TUC). AFL-CIO President John Sweeney was pleased with the decision, stating that 'a majority of the Court has finally and emphatically embraced the simple truth, that the First Amendment abides no law that suppresses independent speech about legislators and candidates, at least absent an explicit call for their election or defeat'.

The likely effect of the ruling will be a significant increase in campaign spending. Supporters of campaign finance regulation bemoaned the Court's decision. 'This is a big win for big money,' stated League of Women Voters President, Mary Wilson. 'Chief Justice Roberts has reopened the door to corruption.'

Freedom of speech

Another case concerning the 1st Amendment's protection of freedom of speech was *Morse* v *Frederick*. The case concerned an incident in Juneau, Alaska, where a high school principal suspended an 18-year-old student, Joseph Frederick, for unfurling a banner reading 'Bong Hits 4 Jesus' as students waited for the Olympic torch to pass through their school in 2002 (a bong is a water pipe commonly used in smoking marijuana). The student claimed that his banner was not advocating drug use and that the school's punishment infringed his 1st Amendment rights.

The Supreme Court, in a 5–4 decision, upheld the school's punishment, saying that school heads could punish students whose speech or demonstration could 'reasonably be viewed' as promoting illegal drug use. Chief Justice Roberts, writing for the majority, stated:

> Student speech celebrating illegal drug use at a school event, in the presence of school administrators and teachers...poses a particular challenge for school officials working to protect those entrusted to their care from the dangers of drug use. The First Amendment does not require schools to tolerate at school events student expression that contributes to those dangers.

Roberts was joined by Justices Scalia, Thomas, Alito and Kennedy, though the latter two made it clear that their concurring votes were given on the understanding that the ruling applied only to the advocacy of illegal drug use.

For the minority, Justice Stevens spoke of 'the Court's ham-handed, categorical approach [that] is deaf to the constitutional imperative to permit unfettered debate, even among high school students, about the wisdom of the war on drugs or of legalising marijuana for medicinal use'. Stevens — the third-oldest person ever to sit on the Supreme Court — harked back to the era of Prohibition, which began 3 months before Stevens was born and ended a month before he turned 13 in 1933. He compared the current ban on marijuana to the abandoned alcohol ban and urged that those who suggest ('however inarticulately') that the ban is 'futile' should be given a fair hearing.

> Just as Prohibition in the 1920s and early 1930s was secretly questioned by thousands of otherwise law-abiding patrons of bootleggers and speakeasies,

today the actions of literally millions of otherwise law-abiding users of marijuana, and the majority of voters in each of the several States that tolerate medicinal uses of the product, lead me to wonder whether the fear of disapproval by those in the majority is silencing opponents of the war on drugs.

And that was written by a Supreme Court justice appointed by Gerald Ford, a Republican president! It just goes to show that the selection of Supreme Court nominees can prove to be a risky business. Ford must have turned in his grave to hear one of his nominees voice such opinions from the highest court in the land, especially after Ford in his autobiography described Stevens's opinions as 'concise, persuasive and legally sound'.

Funding of faith-based organisations

Extract from 1st Amendment (1791)

Congress shall make no law respecting an establishment of religion.

In yet another 5–4 decision, the Supreme Court ruled in *Hein* v *Freedom from Religion Foundation* that federal taxpayers cannot challenge the constitutionality of the Bush administration's policy to assist so-called 'faith-based' organisations — religious-based groups that the White House is keen to include in the delivery of social welfare programmes. The Freedom from Religion Foundation, a Wisconsin-based group of atheists and agnostics, had argued that giving federal money to faith-based groups violated the 1st Amendment provision against the establishment of religion. Liberal groups blasted the Court's decision, while conservative and church groups welcomed it.

Writing for the majority, Justice Samuel Alito — joined by Chief Justice Roberts as well as Justices Scalia, Thomas and Kennedy — argued that 'the payment of taxes is generally not enough to establish standing to challenge an action taken by the federal government'. One can easily see that if the Courts were to allow this link between tax paying and policy deciding, then every taxpayer could sue in the courts to challenge any government expenditure, resulting in the courts being relegated, in the words of Justice Alito, to 'general complaint bureaus'.

Capital punishment

8th Amendment (1791)

Excessive bail shall not be required, nor excessive fines imposed, nor cruel and unusual punishments inflicted.

For the third time in 6 years, the Supreme Court chipped away at the carrying out of the death penalty. In 2002 (*Atkins* v *Virginia*), the Court had declared that the execution of mentally retarded offenders was unconstitutional, as it violated the 8th Amendment ban on 'cruel punishments'. In 2005 (*Roper* v *Simmons*), the Court had declared it unconstitutional to sentence to death someone who had committed a crime when under the age of 18. Now in 2007, in the case of *Panetti* v *Quarterman*, the Supreme Court blocked the execution of a schizophrenic murderer. In yet another 5–4 decision, the Court decided that such executions would violate the 8th Amendment rights of such a person.

Court statistics

In the 2006–07 term, the Supreme Court delivered just 68 opinions, the fewest since the 65 cases decided by the Court in 1952–53. As recently as the early 1990s, the Court was deciding over 100 cases each year. Of the 68 opinions delivered in this term, 24 of them (or 35%) were decided by a margin of 5–4, up from 23% in the previous term and the highest percentage in any recent term. Of these 24 opinions decided by a margin of 5–4, 19 of them were decided along ideological lines, and of these 19 the conservative majority on the Court (led by Chief Justice John Roberts and joined by Associate Justices Antonin Scalia, Clarence Thomas and Samuel Alito) prevailed in 13. The increasingly marginalised liberals on the Court — Justices John Paul Stevens, David Souter, Ruth Bader Ginsburg and Stephen Breyer — prevailed in only six.

Table 4.2 Supreme Court statistics, 2000–07

	2000–01	2001–02	2002–03	2003–04	2004–05	2005–06	2006–07
Number of cases	77	79	71	73	74	69	68
Decided by 5–4 (%)	32	27	20	25	30	23	35
Justice most frequently in majority	O'Connor	O'Connor/ Rehnquist	O'Connor	O'Connor	Breyer	Roberts	Kennedy

Noteworthy was the fact that Justice Anthony Kennedy was in the majority in all 24 of these 5–4 decisions, making him the Justice most frequently in the majority during the 2006–07 term. Indeed, Kennedy was in the majority in 66 of the 68 opinions decided by the Supreme Court (97%). According to Steven Calabresi, professor at Northwestern University School of Law, 'Kennedy is very much the median justice now, as Justice Sandra O'Connor was, and he is to her right.'

The two justices most frequently in agreement were the two new appointees, Roberts and Alito. They agreed on 92% of the Court's non-unanimous cases. The two justices who most frequently disagreed with each other were John Paul Stevens and Clarence Thomas. The two Republican-appointed justices disagreed on 64% of the term's non-unanimous cases.

A more conservative Court

Another conclusion we can draw from this term concerns the relative judicial philosophies of Justices Sandra O'Connor and her replacement Samuel Alito.

US Government & Politics

This was Justice Alito's first full term on the Supreme Court and, according to Linda Greenhouse in *The New York Times* (1 July 2007), he 'is indisputably to Justice O'Connor's right'. What is more, 'his vote in place of hers made the difference in several important cases', including the one to uphold the federal Partial-Birth Abortion Ban Act and to treat campaign advertising by corporations and unions as 'political speech'.

What is more, Justice O'Connor would probably have voted to uphold the school integration plans that the Court, with Justice Alito in the majority, voted to strike down. Indeed, it was Justice O'Connor who wrote the majority opinion in the 2003 case of *Grutter* v *Bollinger*, upholding the affirmative action admission plan at the University of Michigan Law School. No doubt it was this reversal of direction by the Court in just 4 years that prompted Justice Stephen Breyer to remark in his dissent in the 2007 Seattle case that 'it is not often in the law that so few have so quickly changed so much'.

By the end of the Court's term, conservative commentators were trying not to gloat, emphasising the incremental nature of most of the decisions. 'Conservatives got everything they could reasonably have hoped for out of the term,' stated Thomas Goldstein, a Washington lawyer who specialises in Supreme Court litigation. Liberals were clearly distraught. Ralph Neas, president of People for the American Way (the liberal interest group that led the opposition to the appointments of both John Roberts and Samuel Alito) lamented that the current Court 'shows the same respect for precedent that a wrecking ball shows for a plate-glass window'.

Back in 1900, the author Finley Peter Dunne quoted Mr Dooley, his fictional Irish landlord, as saying: 'The Supreme Court follows the election returns.' Mr Dooley's judgement has proved absolutely right in this first decade of the twenty-first century. 'The Supreme Court is a different Court because George W. Bush won the last election and John Kerry did not,' stated legal analyst Jeffrey Toobin. 'That is the beginning and end of the reason why this is a much more conservative Supreme Court than two years ago' ('The Bush Court', *National Journal*, 7 July 2007).

Commentator William Schneider pointed out in the same publication that in several significant cases, a conservative majority that included both Bush appointees — John Roberts and Samuel Alito — changed the Court's previous decisions and directions. In 2000, the old Court threw out a state ban on late-term abortions by a 5–4 vote, but in 2007, the new Court upheld such a ban by 5–4. In 2003, the old Court upheld the Bipartisan Campaign Reform Act by 5–4, but in 2007, in another 5–4 vote, the new Court struck down the section of the law restricting pre-election issue advertising. In 2003, by 5–4, the old Court allowed the use of race as a criterion for admission to schools of higher education. But in 2007, by 5–4, the new Court struck down the use of race as a criterion for placing children in public (state) schools.

What do they think of it so far?

What is the public reaction to all this? In their July 2007 poll, the *Washington Post/ABC News* survey asked three questions relating to the work of the Court. When asked: 'Do you think the Supreme Court tends to be too conservative or too liberal in its decisions, or is it generally balanced?', 31% thought it too conservative, 18% too liberal, while 47% thought it generally balanced. On specific decisions, a minority (40%) approved of the Court's decision on racial balance in schools, but a majority (55%) approved of the Court's upholding of the Partial-Birth Abortion Ban Act.

Other polling evidence suggests that Americans' knowledge of details relating to the Supreme Court is somewhat limited. In a recent AOL-Zogby poll, Americans were asked to name two of the dwarfs in *Snow White and the Seven Dwarfs*. A respectable 77% could do that. But when asked in the same poll to name two of the nine justices of the United States Supreme Court, less than a third could do so.

However, the Gallup polling organisation provided a rather rosier view of the Court. In its May 2007 poll, participants were asked to say whether they approved or disapproved of each of the President, the Congress and the Supreme Court. President Bush managed a 33% approval rating. Congress could muster only 29% — and that figure had fallen to just 18% 3 months later. The Supreme Court, meanwhile, basked in a 51% approval rating, with just 36% disapproving. It is rather ironic that Americans are far more satisfied with members of the federal government, who they do not elect, than with those who they have elected. What lesson, I wonder, should we learn from that?

Questions

1 Explain how both the majority and minority opinions on the Court in the *Gonzales* v *Carhart* decision justified their views. Use some of the extracts from the majority (Justice Kennedy) and minority (Justice Ginsburg) opinions.
2 How did President Bush and House Speaker Pelosi react to the decision?
3 What three reasons does this chapter suggest for regarding the *Gonzales* v *Carhart* decision on abortion rights as such a landmark judgement?
4 Summarise the views of the majority and minority opinions in the *Parents Involved in Community Schools Inc.* v *Seattle School District* case.
5 What effect does the chapter suggest this decision might have on school systems across the United States?
6 Summarise the decision in the case of *FEC* v *Wisconsin Right to Life*.
7 What effect is likely to follow from this judgement?
8 What link did Justice Stevens see between the majority opinion in the case of *Morse* v *Frederick* and the prohibition era in America?
9 Why are Justice Stevens's views so surprising for a judge appointed by a Republican president?
10 What justification did Justice Alito give for the majority opinion in *Hein* v *Freedom from Religion Foundation*?

11 How did the Court further chip away at the death penalty provision in America in its *Panetti* v *Quarterman* decision?
12 Analyse the statistics presented in Table 4.2.
13 What evidence does the chapter present for the current Court being regarded as more conservative since the replacement of Justice O'Connor with Justice Alito?
14 How does the Supreme Court compare with the President and Congress in terms of public approval?

Chapter 5

The Bush presidency in 2007

We know that George W. Bush will leave office at the end of his current term, at noon on 20 January 2009. He is not — and cannot be — a candidate for the presidency in the 2008 presidential election. For almost 150 years, between 1796 and 1940, American presidents adhered to the convention that they would serve only two terms. In 1796, America's first president, George Washington, declined to seek a third term, and his seven successors who found themselves in the same position made the same decision and bowed out after 8 years in the White House: Thomas Jefferson (1808), James Madison (1816), James Munroe (1824), Andrew Jackson (1836), Ulysses Grant (1876), Theodore Roosevelt (1908) and Woodrow Wilson (1920).

In 1940, the Democrat President Franklin Delano Roosevelt broke this tradition. He sought — and won — a third term, and he went on to win a fourth in 1944. He died just a few months into his fourth term on 12 April 1945. When in 1946 the Republicans captured both houses of Congress, they were determined not to see a repeat of the four successive presidential victories. They introduced a constitutional amendment to limit the president to no more than two terms in office. Constitutional amendments require approval by a two-thirds majority in both houses of Congress. Republicans were joined by a number of southern conservative Democrats, who were not great admirers of Roosevelt and his big-government New Deal. The amendment passed through Congress and was duly ratified by the states, becoming the 22nd Amendment in 1951.

Ironically, the first president who was term-limited by this amendment was a Republican, Dwight Eisenhower, who was thereby ineligible to run for a third term in 1960. Another Republican president, Ronald Reagan, was term-limited in 1988, as was Democrat Bill Clinton in 2000. George W. Bush will therefore be the fourth president to be forbidden from running for a third term since the 22nd Amendment was ratified.

In his authoritative book on the presidency (*The American Presidency: A New Perspective*, 1987), James W. Davis wrote that 'most political experts seem agreed that the long-term effects of the [22nd] amendment will undermine the effectiveness of most second-term presidents'. President Truman (1945–53), though excluded from the amendment's ban on third terms, testified to a congressional committee that any elected official who is ineligible for re-election loses political clout. In Truman's words, the American people put their president 'in the hardest job in the world, and send him out to fight with one hand tied behind his back because everyone knows he cannot run for re-election'.

There is a popular view that term limits are undemocratic, because they limit people's choice in an election. Eisenhower in 1960, Reagan in 1988 and Clinton in 2000 all satisfied the constitutional requirements to be president, but voters were not allowed to choose them. There is also a belief that term limits are unnecessary, because elections are in themselves a mechanism to limit terms. As President Truman put it back in the 1940s:

> ...if [the president] is not a good president, and you do not want to keep him, you do not have to re-elect him; there is a way to get rid of him and it does not require a constitutional amendment to do it.

Professor Clinton Rossiter, a leading presidential scholar of his day, predicted 50 years ago — even before the effects of the 22nd Amendment had been seen — that the two-term limit would permanently weaken the presidency: 'Everything in our history tells us that a president who does not and cannot seek re-election loses much of his grip in his last couple of years, and we cannot afford presidents who lose their grip.'

He was right. The 7th and 8th years of the Reagan and Clinton administrations are replete with examples of presidential grip-losing, such as the Iran-Contra Affair for Reagan and the impeachment and trial of Clinton. And for these last 2 years, George W. Bush has likewise suffered from the power-sapping effects of the 22nd Amendment.

A lame duck president?

The term 'lame duck' — used frequently these days to refer to a weakened president in his second term — predates the 22nd Amendment. The first lame ducks waddled onto the political stage nearly 100 years ago, when the *New York Evening Post* first used the term to refer to members of Congress defeated in the 1910 mid-term congressional elections. Today, political commentators do not wait long before conferring lame duck status to a second-term president. The *Houston Chronicle* (the largest newspaper in President Bush's home state of Texas) pronounced the President a lame duck on 20 January 2005, the day he was sworn into office at the start of his second term. The Associated Press got in even more quickly, using the term about President Bush on the day he was re-elected in November 2004.

Any lame duckishness applies only to the *influence* that the president has or does not have during his second term. It does not apply to the *powers* he possesses by virtue of the Constitution. According to James Pfiffner, professor of public policy at George Mason University and one of the most eminent scholars of the presidency: 'President Bush may be a lame duck politically, but he is not a lame duck as chief executive and will lose many of his powers only on 20 January 2009.' In a recent *National Journal* article ('Fowl Territory', 28 July 2007), Professor Pfiffner stated:

> President Bush is still head of the executive branch and commander-in-chief, and has many unilateral powers that he can — and has — used, including executive orders, pardons, control over many regulations, control of executive branch execution of the law, secrecy and classification of documents.

When the Democrat-controlled Congress sends him bills he does not like, he can still veto them, and his veto will almost certainly be sustained. President Bush can still fill vacancies in the federal courts — appointees who by virtue of their life tenure could still be on the bench in two or even three decades' time. Even Democrats agree with this viewpoint: the Democrat chair of the Senate Judiciary Committee, Patrick Leahy, recently went on record as saying: 'No president is ever a lame duck. He's still president.' However, there are certainly signs of lameness in the presidency of George W. Bush. It is informative to try to establish when this political lameness might have begun.

Was it 28 June 2007, when the Senate defeated the Bush-supported immigration bill? The President had just campaigned around the country in support of this legislation and yet, when it came to a vote, only 12 of 49 Republican Senators backed it. Another obvious candidate for Lame Duck Day is 6 November 2006, when voters returned control of both houses of Congress to the Democrats for the first time in 12 years. Or might it have been as early as 27 October 2005? This was the day that Bush's Supreme Court nominee Harriet Miers was forced to withdraw her name from consideration for the vacancy after *Republican* Senators had made it clear that they found her unacceptable. Another contender is 2 September 2005, when the President — while touring Hurricane Katrina-hit Alabama — tried to offer public support to his beleaguered and much-criticised FEMA Director Michael Brown with the words: 'Brownie, you're doing a heckuva job!'

It is not just the fact that in 2007 Bush was in the 7th of his 8 years as president. In 2006, Bush had 55 Republicans in the 100-member Senate; by 2007, he had only 49. In 2006, there were 232 Republicans in the 435-member House of Representatives; the following year he had only 202. In 2006, the President could offer his new cabinet appointees Dirk Kempthorne (Interior), Henry Paulson (Treasury) and Mary Peters (Transportation) at least 2 years in office. When searching for a new Agriculture Secretary in late 2007, there was barely 1 year's work to offer to the would-be nominee. In 2006, the President's approval rating was around the 40% mark, but by September 2007 it was down to 29%.

The consequences of divided government

For the first 6 years in office, George W. Bush had the significant advantage of having both houses of Congress controlled by his fellow Republicans. (There was an 18-month period, between mid-2001 and the end of 2002, when the Democrats controlled the Senate, but this was mostly at a time when the President was so popular — post 9/11 — that it hardly mattered anyway.) Not since President Eisenhower, in 1953, had a Republican president enjoyed a party majority in both houses of Congress, and Eisenhower had that majority for only 2 years. The last Republican president to have 6 or more years of his own party in control of both houses of Congress was Theodore Roosevelt, between 1901 and 1909.

However, as a consequence of the 2006 mid-term elections, the Democrats regained control of both the House (233–202) and the Senate (51–49). And so George W. Bush had to face 'divided government' for the last 2 years of his second term. This always makes life more difficult for the president, whether he is looking to get his bills passed, his budgets approved, his vetoes sustained, his appointments confirmed or his treaties ratified.

Democrat Bill Clinton faced enormous difficulties in getting his 1995 budget approved by a Republican-controlled Congress. In the same year, Congress overrode Clinton's veto of the Securities Bill. In 1997, the Republican-controlled Senate refused to confirm Clinton's nominee William Weld as ambassador to Mexico, and in 1999 they rejected his nominee Ronnie White as a federal trial court judge. It is tough being president with divided government, as many of George W. Bush's predecessors can testify. His three immediate predecessors — Reagan (between 1987 and 1989), his father George H. W. Bush (for the whole of his one-term presidency, 1989–93) and Bill Clinton (between 1995 and 2001) — all suffered the same fate.

Filling cabinet vacancies

Presidents never find filling cabinet posts easy, not even at the beginning of an administration. There are numerous stories told of people simply saying 'no' to the president when offered a job in the cabinet. But as the end of the president's second term of office comes ever closer, cabinet recruitment becomes ever more difficult.

By the close of 2007, George W. Bush had made a total of 33 appointments to head the 15 executive departments of the federal government. Of those, 14 were appointments made at the beginning of his first term and one was to head the newly created Department of Homeland Security in March 2003. The remaining 18 constituted 'replacement' appointments, these being appointments to fill vacancies that occur during a presidential term. As shown in Table 5.1, this represents a figure on the high side of cabinet appointments. President Reagan made 20 replacement cabinet appointments in 8 years (1981–89) and Nixon made 19 in just over 5 years (1969–74). One would also expect George W. Bush to make further replacement cabinet appointments in 2008. In their final years in office, Ronald Reagan had to make three cabinet appointments and Bill Clinton two.

Table 5.1 Cabinet appointments made by presidents, 1961–2007

	Kennedy	Johnson	Nixon	Ford	Carter	Reagan	Bush	Clinton	Bush
Original	10	0	12	0	11	13	14	14	14
New department	0	2	0	0	2	0	0	0	1
Replacement	3	13	19	12	8	20	8	16	18
Total	13	15	31	12	21	33	22	30	33

Presidents who are nearing the end of their tenure tend to make appointments from within the federal government rather than trying to recruit from outside. It becomes much harder to attract people into an executive branch job when so little time of a president's final term remains. There is likely to be the temptation to shuffle up the number two in a department to replace the boss.

That option, however, was not available when Alberto Gonzales resigned from the Justice Department as Attorney General in August 2007. Gonzales was forced to resign following his unsatisfactory answers to allegations that he had been responsible for firing nine US attorneys for political reasons. By the time Gonzales announced his resignation, the department's number two (Deputy Attorney General Paul McNulty) and number three (Associate Attorney General William Mercer) had already quit. The President may have liked to nominate another Justice Department insider, former Solicitor General Theodore Olson, but the Senate Majority Leader Harry Reid had vowed to block the nomination. This is an example of the power of the Senate to influence presidential nominations to the executive branch of the federal government.

Three weeks after Gonzales's resignation, President Bush announced that he was nominating a 66-year-old former federal judge, Michael Mukasey of New York, to be the new Attorney General. Mukasey had been appointed to the federal bench in 1987 by President Reagan, where he served for nearly 20 years, the last 6 years as chief judge. He had presided over the trial of Omar Abdel Rahman, an Egyptian cleric charged with plotting to destroy a number of New York City landmarks, including the World Trade Center, in February 1993.

Mukasey's nomination was initially greeted with bipartisan approval. However, during his confirmation hearings in front of the Senate Judiciary Committee in late October, Mukasey gave what many Democrats regarded as unsatisfactory answers to questions about the use by the US government of a simulated drowning technique known as 'waterboarding' when interrogating terrorist suspects. Mukasey angered many Democrats by refusing to call such a practice illegal. When the Senate Judiciary Committee voted on Mukasey's nomination on 6 November, it recommended approval by 11 votes to 8. All nine Republicans on the committee, plus two Democrats — Dianne Feinstein and Charles Schumer — voted 'yes', while the remaining eight Democrats voted 'no'. The following week, Mukasey was confirmed by the full Senate by a vote of 53 to 40.

During 2007, President Bush had two more cabinet vacancies to fill. On 17 July, Veterans Affairs Secretary Jim Nicholson suddenly announced his resignation after mounting criticism of poor healthcare provision for veterans injured in the Iraq war. Nicholson, a former Republican National Committee chair and a Vietnam veteran, had served as Veterans Affairs Secretary for only 2 years. On 30 October, the President announced that he was nominating Dr James Peake to the post. Peake is a distinguished former army general and physician, the first of both categories to head up the department.

In mid-September, Agriculture Secretary Michael Johanns announced his departure from the Bush cabinet. Johanns intends to run for the open Senate seat in his native state of Nebraska, following the announcement by Republican Senator Chuck Hagel that he would not seek a third term in 2008. Johanns had previously served as Mayor of Lincoln (1991–99) and was Governor of Nebraska from 1999 until he was recruited by President Bush as Agriculture Secretary in 2005. To replace Johanns, Bush chose Ed Schafer, the former Governor of North Dakota. Schafer becomes the sixth former state Governor to serve in George W. Bush's cabinet.

Approval ratings — more like Nixon than Clinton

President Bush began his second term in January 2005 with a 52% approval rating (see Figure 5.1). It reached a peak of 57% (4–6 February) but then slipped quickly into the mid-40 percents by the middle of that year, where it remained. By the spring of 2006, the President's approval rating had fallen even further, reaching as low as 31% in early May. It is at this point that the figures have stuck throughout 2006 and 2007, hitting an all-time low of 29% in July 2007. This was the lowest approval rating for any modern-day president in the third July of their second term, worse than Harry Truman's 32% in 1951. For comparison, in July 1999, just months before his impeachment, Bill Clinton had a 60% approval rating. From an average approval rating of 71% in 2002, Bush fell to an average of 34% in 2007.

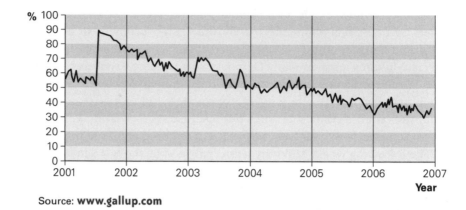

Source: **www.gallup.com**

Figure 5.1 President George W. Bush's approval ratings, January 2001–September 2007

Table 5.2 shows how these figures fit into the historical setting of postwar presidents. Bush's 29% approval rating in July 2007 was as low as his father's rating in July 1992, but not quite as low as Jimmy Carter's in June 1979 or Richard Nixon's in the month before he resigned in 1974.

Table 5.2 Presidential job approval low points: Truman to Bush

President	Lowest approval rating (%)	Date
John F. Kennedy	56	September 1963
Dwight D. Eisenhower	49	July 1960
Gerald Ford	37	March 1975
Bill Clinton	37	June 1993
Ronald Reagan	35	January 1983
Lyndon Johnson	35	August 1968
George H. W. Bush	29	July 1992
George W. Bush	29	July 2007
Jimmy Carter	28	June 1979
Richard Nixon	24	July/August 1974
Harry Truman	22	February 1952

Source: **www.gallup.com**

Low approval ratings for a president have political consequences. In 2002, with his approval ratings in the 70% bracket, President Bush was being sought by almost every Republican candidate for support in that year's mid-term elections. In 5 days, the President travelled 16,000 kilometres, visiting 17 cities in 15 different states. According to a report in the *Washington Post,* the Republican Senate candidate in Georgia, Saxby Chambliss 'implored President Bush to jet to his state and fire up potential voters'. Five years later, Republican Senator Susan Collins was asked if she would like to get fundraising help from the President for her 2008 re-election bid. Her answer was less than definite:

Oh, jeez, I don't anticipate — well, who knows? I really haven't focused on that, but my general view is, anyone who legally wants to help raise money…

Five years in politics is a *very* long time.

Few policy achievements

Low approval ratings also make it difficult for a president to have much political clout. It diminishes his persuasive power, especially on Capitol Hill. This was seen in the President's failure to secure immigration reform legislation in June 2007, despite his personal campaign for it. A search of the White House website shows the President making numerous appearances, visits and speeches pushing his immigration reform package (see Table 5.3). But on 28 June, immigration reform was defeated in Congress. 'A lot of us worked hard to see if we couldn't find a common ground,' said the President just an hour after immigration reform died on Capitol Hill. 'It didn't work.'

It did not work either on social security reform, another big-ticket item on Bush's second-term agenda. And when the report that the President commissioned on tax reform proved too provocative, Bush shelved it. Curbs on excessive litigation were another item on Bush's to-do list. Though he has managed to get Congress to pass limits on class-action lawsuits, the remainder of Bush's proposals — most notably to restrict medical malpractice awards — has gone nowhere. By 2007, Bush's domestic agenda was limited to persuading Congress to re-authorise his Education Reform Act of 2001 (the so-called 'No Child Left Behind' programme) and trying to stop Congress from expanding a children's health insurance programme (SCHIP).

Table 5.3 President Bush's appearances regarding immigration reform,
9 April–28 June 2007

Date (2007)	Presidential event
9 April	Discusses immigration reform in Yuma, Arizona
3 May	Discusses immigration reform with clergy in Washington DC
4 May	Discusses immigration reform at Rose Garden event
19 May	Speaks about immigration reform in weekly radio address
29 May	Discusses immigration reform in Glynco, Georgia
1 June	Holds press briefing on immigration reform
14 June	Discusses immigration reform with Associated Builders and Contractors Convention, Capitol Hilton Hotel, Washington DC
26 June	White House press conference on immigration reform
28 June	Makes statement that he is disappointed in Congress's failure to pass immigration reform

Source: **www.whitehouse.gov**

Leadership by veto

Leadership by veto looked to be where the President was pinning his hopes in 2007. Bush vetoed no legislation for the first 66 months of his presidency — well into his second term — thereby becoming the first president to serve a full 4-year term without vetoing a single piece of legislation since John Quincy Adams' first term (1825–29). Many Republicans had been disappointed that the President had not used his veto power more aggressively during the earlier years of his administration. Given that the veto is what could be described as 'the-president-nearly-always-wins' power (Congress overrides only a fraction of all vetoes), it is hard to see why the President has not made more use of this power. Bush did then use the power once in 2006 to veto the Stem Cell Research Enhancement Bill.

On 1 May 2007, Bush vetoed a second bill, the Iraq Accountability Bill, which would have set a deadline for the withdrawal of American troops from Iraq. In his veto message to Congress with the returned bill, the President stated:

> I am returning herewith without my approval the US Troop Readiness, Veterans' Care, Katrina Recovery and Iraq Accountability Appropriations Act, 2007. This legislation is objectionable because it would set an arbitrary date for beginning the withdrawal of American troops without regard to conditions on the ground; it would micromanage the commanders in the field by restricting their ability to direct the fight in Iraq; and it contains billions of dollars of spending and other provisions completely unrelated to the war.

Congress had no chance of overriding the President's veto, which requires a two-thirds majority in both houses. The final passage votes had been 218–208 in the House and 51–46 in the Senate. The day after the President vetoed the legislation, the House did attempt to override the veto but failed with a vote of 222–203, which was 62 votes short of the 284 votes required. In this override vote, there were two Republicans who voted 'yes' and seven Democrats who voted 'no'.

Six weeks later, on 20 June 2007, President Bush again vetoed a Stem Cell Research Enhancement Bill, almost identical to the legislation he vetoed in 2006. The bill would have provided federal funding for stem cell research, in effect overturning the restrictions he imposed on funding shortly after he became president in 2001. The Senate had passed the bill at the Third Reading on 11 April by 63 votes to 34. Two Democrats voted 'no' and 17 Republicans voted 'yes'. On 7 June, the House passed an identical bill 247–176. Again, this was pretty much a party-line vote, but with 16 Democrats voting 'no' and 37 Republicans voting 'yes'. Both votes were short of the two-thirds majority that would have been required to override the veto, though the Senate vote was only two votes short. However, neither chamber attempted to override Bush's veto.

The fourth Bush veto took place on 3 October, this time of the bipartisan State Children's Health Insurance Programme (SCHIP) Bill. Despite the fact that on final passage 45 Republicans in the House and 18 Republicans in the Senate supported the bill, the President issued his promised veto. Bush opposed the bill because he regarded it as far too expensive. He had proposed a compromise back in February that would have resulted in far lower costs. The President claimed that the vetoed bill was so generous in its provision of child health insurance that 'a family of four earning almost $83,000 a year' would qualify for SCHIP aid, meaning that 'one of out of every three children moving onto government coverage would be moving from private coverage', rather than from no coverage at all, which was the original intention of the SCHIP legislation. However, once again, Congress failed to override the President's veto: the vote in the House was 273–156, 13 votes short of the necessary two-thirds majority.

Bush suffered his first veto override on 8 November 2007. The legislation concerned was the Water Resources Development Act, which both Houses had passed by huge majorities earlier in the year. Despite the fact that only 40 House members and 12 Senators opposed the Bill on final passage, Bush vetoed it on 2 November. In his veto message Bush accused the Democrat Congress of passing a Bill that 'lacks fiscal discipline'. However, on 6 November, the House voted to override the veto by 361–54, a whacking 84 votes over the required two-thirds majority. A total of 138 Republicans voted to override Bush's veto. Two days later, the Senate voted 79–14 to override the veto, 17 votes above the 62 votes required. Not a single Senator spoke for the President's position in the final debate. It was the first time that Congress had overridden a presidential veto since February 1998.

Table 5.4 George W. Bush's vetoes, 2001–07

Bill	Final passage votes		Veto	Override votes		Result
	House	Senate		House	Senate	
Stem Cell Research	238–194	63–37	19 July 2006	235–193	—	Sustained
Iraq Accountability	218–208	51–46	1 May 2007	222–203	—	Sustained
Stem Cell Research	247–176	63–34	20 July 2007	—	—	Sustained
Child's Health Insurance	265–149	67–29	3 October 2007	273–156	—	Sustained
Water Resources Development	381–40	81–12	2 November 2007	361–54	79–14	Overridden
Labor, HSS, Education Spending	274–141	56–37	13 November 2007	277–141	—	Sustained

Presidential character

Throughout much of 2007, despite gloomy news from Capitol Hill and Baghdad and the loss of his close friend Alberto Gonzales from the Department of Justice, Bush seemed surprisingly at ease with himself. But if

Bush does not seem worried, others are. Writing in the *Washington Post* on 2 July 2007, political correspondent Peter Baker wrote:

> Burdened by an unrelenting war, challenged by an opposition Congress, defeated on immigration reform, Bush remains largely locked inside the fortress of 1600 Pennsylvania Avenue. He still travels, making speeches to friendly audiences and attending summit meetings. But he rarely goes out to dinner, and he no longer plays golf, except occasionally chipping at Camp David, where, as at his Texas ranch, he can find refuge.

'I don't know how he copes with it,' said Donald Ensenat, a friend for 43 years who recently stepped down as State Department protocol officer. Representative Michael Conaway (Republican–Texas), another long-time friend who once worked for Bush, said he looks worn down:

> It's a marked difference in his physical appearance. It's an incredibly heavy load. When you ask men and women to take risks, to send them into war knowing they might not come home, that's got to be an incredible burden to have on your shoulders.

Bad news has come on the Bush administration like an unrelenting snow storm in the past few years: social security reform, Iraq, Hurricane Katrina, Harriet Miers, Jack Abramoff, Tom DeLay, Mark Foley, the 2006 mid-term elections, Lewis 'Scooter' Libby, Donald Rumsfeld, Alberto Gonzales, Larry Craig, Paul Wolfowitz, immigration reform. No president since Harry Truman has had such low approval ratings over such a long period. Even Richard Nixon did not fall below a 50% approval rating until just over a year before he resigned.

How does Bush react? Is he like Lyndon Johnson, who was tormented by the daily chanting of anti-Vietnam War protesters: 'Hey, hey, LBJ, how many kids did you kill today?' Is he like Richard Nixon, who sank into self-pity and isolation as the Watergate net closed around him? Or is he like Bill Clinton, who fumed with anger against his Republican enemies and that 'vast, right-wing conspiracy' that climaxed with his impeachment? Bush is not, in fact, a tormented Johnson, a self-pitying Nixon, or an angry Clinton. Henry Kissinger, who as Secretary of State spent much time with President Nixon during the twilight days of his presidency, says that George W. Bush (to whom he acts as an unofficial adviser) is 'serene', adding: 'I know President Johnson was railing against his fate. But that's not the case with Bush. He feels he's doing what he needs to do, and he seems to me at peace with himself.'

But what is resolve and inner peace to some is to others a loss of reality. Some see the President as isolated, taking advice from an ever-decreasing circle of close friends and confidants. 'There's nobody [in the White House] who can stand up to him and tell him, "Mr President, you've got to do this.

You're wrong on this." There's no adult supervision. It's like he's oblivious,' commented one senior House Republican to a *Washington Post* reporter.

Bush has taken to reading biographies, including ones on George Washington and Winston Churchill. He has held private seminars with leading historians, including the leading British academic Alistair Horne. Kissinger had given the President a copy of Horne's book *A Savage War of Peace*, which is about the French defeat in Algeria in the 1950s. Having read the book, Bush invited Horne to the White House. While Horne is no Bush supporter, he was hugely struck by the President's tranquillity: 'My God, he looked well. He looked like he came off a cruise in the Caribbean. He looked like he didn't have a care in the world. It was amazing.'

The President continues to draw much on his faith as a committed Christian. 'His faith is very strong,' comments Michael Novak, a scholar at the American Enterprise Institute. 'He seeks guidance in prayer. And that means trying to be sure he's doing the right thing. And if you've got that set, all the criticism, it doesn't faze you very much.'

But as the final months and weeks of his presidency loom, Bush will find it hard not to feel increasingly lonely and isolated. Cabinet members are leaving, and so are some of his most trusted White House aides, including Chief of Staff Andrew Card, Counselor to the President Dan Bartlett and Press Secretary Tony Snow. Neither can the President any longer count on the loyalty of Republicans in Congress. With approval ratings around the 30% mark, the President becomes pretty toxic. He has been criticised by a number of Republicans in Congress for his conduct of the Iraq War, his holding on to Attorney General Alberto Gonzales for too long, and for his veto of the Stem Cell Research and SCHIP Bills.

Conclusion

Second terms are rarely political successes. Bush clearly over-egged the pudding in the euphoria of his 2004 re-election: just 2 days afterwards, he offered this view of the political landscape as he saw it:

> I feel it necessary to move an agenda that I told the American people I would move. I earned capital in the campaign, political capital, and now I intend to spend it. It's my style. I've earned capital in this election — and I'm going to spend it for what I told the American people I'd spend it on, which is Social Security and tax reform, moving this economy forward, education, fighting and winning the war on terror.

He might have done better to be a little more modest. But David Broder, the much respected political commentator of the *Washington Post*, discovered that the Bush White House believed that the bigger and bolder the goals they set for themselves, the more they would achieve. And unlike Clinton in 1997, Reagan in 1985, Nixon in 1973 and Eisenhower in 1957, Bush in 2005 was beginning his second term with his own party in the majority in both houses of Congress. That hadn't happened since Harry Truman in 1949. The noted academic George C. Edwards concluded (in *Governing by Campaigning*, 2006) that 'Bush began his second term by substantially overestimating his political capital and overreaching with a bold and aggressive programme of reform.' According to Charles O. Jones, writing in a volume entitled *Second-Term Blues: How George W. Bush Has Governed* (2007), Bush saw his re-election in 2004 as an endorsement of his policies:

> In his mind, his election victory [in 2004] provided affirmation, not only of him but also of Congress. He saw his campaign as asking 'Should I do these things?' The voters said yes. What about co-operating with Democrats? The President provided a classic executive response: 'With the campaign over, Americans are expecting a bipartisan effort and results. I'll reach out to everyone who shares our goals.' That is about as tightly argued as a rationale can be: I won. You lost. That's behind us. Let's get down to work on the winning programme — mine.

One was beginning to get an idea of the President's loss of political clout by taking an early look at his support score in the House of Representatives during the first 10 months of 2007. By the end of October 2007, there had been 1,026 votes on the floor of the House of Representatives — already a record, easily beating the 885 votes during the whole of 1995. Of those 1,026 votes, the President had taken a clear position on 95. But he had won only 12 of those 95 votes, representing a support score of just under 13%, the lowest level registered since the statistics were first published in 1953. The previous lowest was the 26% Clinton recorded in the House in 1995. Compare that with Bush's support score in the House of Representatives in 2006 of 85%.

Presidential scholar Fred Greenstein of Princeton University has commented that for President Bush 'the sand is flowing out of the hour glass'. The eighth year of a presidency (2008) is rarely, if ever, an opportunity for great legislative achievements, especially for a president who faces the twin difficulties of a Congress controlled by the opposition party and lethally low approval ratings. But it is far too early to write the Bush legacy just yet. Anything could happen to change the political landscape of the Bush administration, such as another attack on the US mainland, the capture of Osama bin Laden or a sudden deterioration of the situation in Iraq. As stated at this chapter's opening, barring unforeseen accidents, George W. Bush does not leave office until 12 noon on 20 January 2009. There's quite some way to go yet.

Questions

1 Explain how and why the 22nd Amendment came to be passed.
2 Which presidents have been ineligible to run for a third term as a result of this amendment?
3 President Harry Truman, as well as academics such as James W. Davis and Clinton Rossiter, all agreed about the likely effects of this amendment. Explain what their views were and state whether you think that their opinions have proved to be correct.
4 Explain the meaning and origins of the term 'lame duck president'.
5 Give two examples of when President Bush might first have been regarded as a 'lame duck president'.
6 Explain the term 'divided government'. Give some examples of previous presidents who had difficulties with Congress in a period of divided government.
7 Write a paragraph about why Alberto Gonzales resigned as Attorney General and the process for choosing and confirming his successor.
8 How did President Bush's approval ratings in 2007 compare with those of his predecessors?
9 What are the consequences for a president of low approval ratings?
10 Write a paragraph about George W. Bush's vetoing of legislation concerning stem cell research and the State Children's Health Insurance Programme (SCHIP).
11 How does Bush react to the difficulties he faced in 2007?
12 How successful was Bush in getting what he wanted in the House of Representatives in the first 10 months of 2007? How did this compare with 2006?

Chapter 6

President Ford (1913–2006): healer or failure?

At noon on 9 August 1974, Gerald R. Ford (who had never before been elected to anything outside his Michigan congressional district) was sworn in as the 38th president of the United States. It was the culmination of the most extraordinary set of circumstances ever to befall the American presidency.

Ford had never sought national office. As a Republican congressman, he might have aspired to become Speaker of the House of Representatives, but his party was in a clear minority in the House — and had been for 20 years — so Ford had settled for House Minority Leader. What events propelled a somewhat anonymous congressman to the Oval Office? How did Ford rise to the occasion? Was his brief tenure — just 29 months — adjudged a success or a failure?

Gerald Ford died on 26 December 2006 at the age of 93, nearly 30 years after relinquishing the presidency in January 1977. This affords as good a moment as any to offer an assessment of his time in office. (An assessment of the presidency of Ronald Reagan appeared in the 2006 edition of this *Annual Survey* and an assessment of Bill Clinton appears in chapter 6 of Anthony J. Bennett's *The Presidency and Presidential Power*, also published by Philip Allan Updates in 2006.)

Early life in Washington politics

The man we know as Gerald Ford was born Leslie King on 14 July 1913 in Omaha, Nebraska, the offspring of an affluent home but a failed marriage. His parents divorced the following January and his mother, Dorothy King, returned to her parental home in Grand Rapids, Michigan, where she married Gerald Ford, a young paint salesman she met at a church social. He formally adopted her child, who was renamed Gerald R. Ford Jr.

Ford entered politics in 1948, the year Harry Truman was elected president. Ford was elected to represent Michigan's 5th congressional district, centred on his home town of Grand Rapids; he represented the district for the next 25 years, making him the president with the longest congressional service in the history of the presidency. In the same year, Ford married Elizabeth Warren, and thus the Fords arrived in Washington in the winter of 1948–49 to begin a lifetime of Washington politics.

Writing in the *Washington Post* obituary in December 2006, Lou Cannon wrote of Ford that he quickly established himself as a diligent and popular district-service congressman who 'answered every letter and made himself available to visitors from his state'. Ford was popular with his colleagues and quickly won an assignment to the prestigious House Appropriations Committee. In foreign policy, Ford was an internationalist, supporting Democrat Harry Truman's famous 'plan' of aid to underdeveloped countries.

By 1960, *Newsweek* magazine rated him second among the ablest members of Congress, and Ford was elected to the House Republican leadership in 1963. It was in this capacity that Ford showed his abilities at friendly persuasion, not only of fellow Republicans, but of Democrats too. 'It's the damnedest thing,' remarked Joe Waggonner (Democrat–Louisiana). 'Jerry [Ford] just puts his arm around a colleague or looks him in the eye, says, "I need your vote", and gets it.' Such persuasive abilities would be exceedingly useful as president.

Following the assassination of President Kennedy in November 1963, President Johnson appointed Ford to the Warren Commission, set up to investigate the circumstances surrounding the assassination. It was during the same time, however, that Ford became the butt of a much-popularised — and, many thought, both unfair and unkind — jibe by President Johnson that Ford was so intellectually limited that he couldn't 'chew gum and walk at the same time'. Ford merely laughed off this and similar jibes.

Ideologically, Ford was known as a moderate Republican — on foreign policy as well as on domestic issues, such as civil rights. But in 1970, Ford seemed briefly to abandon such moderation in leading the charge to impeach the noted liberal US Supreme Court Justice William Douglas. In the course of this matter, Ford offered a definition (often quoted during the Clinton impeachment proceedings in the late 1990s) of what constitutes an impeachable offence. 'What then is an impeachable offence?', Ford asked in a speech in April 1970. 'The only honest answer is that an impeachable offence is whatever the majority of the House of Representatives considers it to be at any given moment in history.'

Chosen as vice-president

When President Kennedy was assassinated in November 1963, Vice-President Johnson immediately became president. But the vice-presidency remained vacant until after the 1964 election. There was no provision for filling vice-presidential vacancies. In 1967, the 25th Amendment to the Constitution was passed, providing that if the vice-presidential office became vacant for any reason, then the president should nominate a new vice-president, with his choice being confirmed by a simple majority vote of both houses of Congress.

On 10 October 1973, Vice-President Spiro Agnew pleaded 'no contest' in a federal courtroom to charges of income tax evasion and resigned from office. Later that evening, Gerald Ford was at his home in Alexandria, Virginia, on the edge of Washington DC when the phone rang. It was his old former House friend Melvin Laird, who now worked in the Nixon White House. He had rung to ask Ford whether he would be interested in the vice-presidency. 'I suspect if I was asked, I would accept it,' Ford replied. The next evening it was President Nixon who telephoned the Ford home and offered him the job.

By this time, President Nixon was deeply embroiled in what had become known as the Watergate affair. Ford took on trust what he was told privately by the White House: that the President was innocent of any involvement in the affair or in any attempt to cover up the conspiracy. In the end, of course, this trust proved widely misplaced.

Ford was quickly and easily confirmed by both houses of Congress: by 92–3 in the Senate and by 387–35 by the House. And so, on 6 December 1973, Ford became Vice-President of the United States, and next in line to the presidency.

Ford as president

Exactly 8 months later, on 6 August 1974, President Nixon assembled his cabinet for what would be the last time. Nixon had now been shown to have lied about Watergate — he had instigated and carried out an elaborate cover-up and had told numerous lies to political friends and foes alike. Seated opposite Nixon across the massive cabinet table, Ford told the President: 'I can no longer publicly defend you.' As Adam Clymer commented in Ford's *New York Times* obituary (27 December 2006), 'it was for Mr Ford, the loyal friend of the President, one of the most difficult things he had ever done,' but, as Ford told an interviewer some time later, 'with the development of the evidence, I had no other choice'.

Two nights later, Nixon appeared on television announcing his imminent resignation — the first US president to resign from office. And at noon on 9 August 1974, Ford became president, having been elected neither as vice-president nor as president. The nation, bitterly divided over Watergate as well as the conduct of the Vietnam war, needed healing. Ford tried to begin this healing process in a brief but memorable inaugural address, delivered not as usual at an elaborately staged outdoor ceremony at the Capitol, but at a hastily arranged indoor ceremony in the White House.

Ford spoke to the nation for the first time as their president:

> My fellow Americans, our long national nightmare is over. Our Constitution works. Our great republic is a government of laws and not of men. Here the people rule.

The 'long national nightmare' was Watergate, to which he made further references in the speech, along with a direct appeal for healing:

> As we bind up the internal wounds of Watergate, more painful and more poisonous than those of foreign wars, let us restore the golden rule to our political process and let brotherly love purge our hearts of suspicion and hate.

Ford wanted to end the atmosphere of the Nixon years, during which time the President had lied and betrayed the trust that so many — including Ford — had placed in him. Ford stated that: 'I believe that truth is the glue that holds government together.'

He then addressed the issue of his never having been elected to national office, either as vice-president or now as president. He continued:

> I am acutely aware that you have not elected me as your president by your ballots. So I ask you to confirm me as your president with your prayers. I have not sought this enormous responsibility, but I will not shirk it.

Americans rallied round their new president and Ford basked in approval ratings in the 70% range.

The Nixon pardon

The honeymoon was brief: it lasted precisely a month, ended by Ford's sudden announcement that he was going to pardon former President Nixon. This is how Ford himself, in his autobiography *A Time to Heal* (1979), tells of the pardon announcement that early September Sunday morning:

> Once I determine to move, I seldom, if ever, fret. I have confidence that my lifetime batting average is high, and I'm prepared to live with the consequences. Still, I wanted to go to church and pray for guidance and understanding before making the announcement. So at 8 o'clock Sunday morning (8 September), I attended a service at St John's Episcopal Church on Lafayette Square. I sat alone in the presidential pew, took Holy Communion and then returned to the Oval Office. Just before 11 o'clock, the TV cameramen and sound technicians entered the Oval Office. Soon after I saw the red light just below the camera flash on, and I began to read.

What the President read was a prepared statement he had already shared with his closest White House aides and congressional leaders:

> Ladies and gentlemen, I have come to a decision which I felt I should tell you and all of my fellow American citizens as soon as I was certain in my own mind and in my own conscience that it is the right thing to do...After years of bitter controversy and divisive national debate, I have been advised and I am compelled to conclude that many months and perhaps more years will have to pass before Richard Nixon could obtain a fair trial by jury in any jurisdiction of the United States. During this long period of delay and protracted litigation, ugly passions would again be aroused, and our people would again be polarised in their opinions...

> My conscience tells me clearly and certainly that I cannot prolong the bad dreams that continue to reopen a chapter that is closed. My conscience tells me that only I, as President, have the constitutional power to firmly shut and seal

this book…Now, therefore, I, Gerald R. Ford, President of the United States, pursuant to the pardon power conferred on me by Article II, Section 2, of the Constitution, have granted and by these presents do grant a full, free and absolute pardon unto Richard Nixon for all offences against the United States which he, Richard Nixon, has committed or may have committed or taken part in during the period from January 20, 1969, through August 9, 1974.

Ford continues in his memoir:

I signed the pardon proclamation. Finally, it was done. It was an unbeliev-able lifting of a burden from my shoulders. I felt very certain that I had made the right decision.

Others, however, did not share the President's confidence. The pardon announcement was received with a firestorm of criticism. Even his own White House press secretary, Jerry terHorst, resigned rather than defend the President's decision. Ford's popularity ratings slumped overnight. His harshest critics accused him of having done a deal with Nixon: the presidency for a pardon. Ford categorically and emphatically denied that there was any such deal. He even broke with tradition and agreed to appear before a congressional committee on the matter. Appearing before the House Judiciary Subcommittee on Criminal Justice in October 1974, the President stated: 'I want to assure you, the members of this subcommittee, members of Congress, the American people, there was no deal, period, under no circumstances.'

Ford never had regrets over the pardon. Interviewed after he left office, Ford commented:

I felt then, and I feel now, if I was going to do it, it had to be done clean, sudden. It was part of the healing process. It didn't turn out to be quite as much of a healing at the time!

But at least one of his fiercest critics did, over time, change his mind about the Nixon pardon. Senator Edward Kennedy (Democrat–Massachusetts) was one of the most vocal critics of the pardon in 1974. In May 2001, when Gerald Ford was awarded a 'Profile in Courage' Award at the John F. Kennedy Library in Boston, Senator Edward Kennedy spoke of how he had originally opposed the pardon. 'But time has a way of clarifying past events,' he said, 'and now we see that President Ford was right.'

In 1999, Bob Woodward — the *Washington Post* reporter who broke and then pursued the Watergate story and was, at the time, a critic of the pardon — wrote in his book *Shadow: Five Presidents and the Legacy of Watergate*:

As the years have passed, I have become more and more convinced that Ford made the correct decision in pardoning Nixon. Nixon had already paid the political death penalty of resignation, and for Ford a pardon was the only way of ending the public and media obsession with his predecessor's future.

Continuing bad news

The first full year of Ford's presidency, 1975, was to be a bleak year. In their State of the Union Address, presidents are almost always upbeat. Not so President Ford in 1975:

> I must say to you that the state of the Union is not good. Millions of Americans are out of work. Recession and inflation are eroding the money of millions more. Prices are too high and sales are too slow.

To try to tackle rampant inflation, the President came up with a 32-point package of measures to cut taxes and control spending. He described inflation as 'public enemy number one'. The slogan was 'Whip Inflation Now' and was popularised (if that's the correct word) by red badges bearing the acronym 'WIN'. When New York City went bankrupt, the President's initial response was to refuse any further economic assistance to a city that the President saw as badly and wastefully managed — by Democrats. The famous New York *Daily Post* headline read: 'FORD TO CITY: DROP DEAD'.

Ford was faced with huge Democrat majorities in both houses of Congress. The Republicans had done badly in the 1974 mid-term elections, losing five seats in the Senate and 48 in the House. The President was thus reduced to government by veto. He vetoed 17 bills in 1975 alone, more than President Johnson had vetoed in his 5 years in the White House.

There was little relief in foreign policy. In April, South Vietnam finally fell to the Communists, Congress having refused Ford any further money for continuing the unpopular war. Three days before Saigon (the capital of South Vietnam) fell to the Communists, Ford ordered the evacuation by helicopter of the remaining Americans. But the picture of the airlift from the American Embassy roof came to symbolise, for many, a humiliating withdrawal.

Ford felt constrained by the recently passed War Powers Act (1973), which sought to restrict the president's use of troops without prior and specific congressional authorisation. Ford and his White House successors have regarded the legislation as unconstitutional, violating the president's powers as commander-in-chief. Unlike his successors, Ford felt in a weak position with no electoral mandate. He did, however, voice his belief that having Congress running the minutiae of foreign policy was neither sensible, nor in accordance with the wishes of the Founding Fathers. Speaking during his 1976 re-election campaign, Ford would state: 'Our forefathers knew you could not have 535 commanders-in-chief and secretaries of state. It just wouldn't work.'

When in May 1975 Cambodian Communists seized the US merchant ship the *Mayaguez* with its crew of 39, Ford reacted with decisiveness, sending military forces to recapture the ship. Even his critics were mildly and temporarily impressed that the crisis was over in 65 hours, and Ford's approval ratings rose by 11 points. Less well received was his signing of the Helsinki Accords on human rights with the Soviet leader Leonid Brezhnev. Ford's critics, who included from within his own party Ronald Reagan, the former Governor of California, believed that the accords merely legitimised the Cold War boundaries in Europe, while glossing over human rights abuses both in the Soviet Union and its satellite states.

September brought two assassination attempts on Ford's life, both by women. Neither succeeded in firing, but both went to jail for life for their attempts. Before the year's end, Ford decided the White House organisation needed a shake-up. He appointed a new White House Chief of Staff — a 34-year-old by the name of Dick Cheney.

Election year

In 1976, Ford decided to seek election to the presidency in his own right. Before he could do that, he had to see off a serious challenge from a candidate on the right of the Republican Party, Ronald Reagan. An incumbent president would normally be awarded the nomination of his own party without a fight, but these were not conventional times. Conservative Republicans regarded Ford as too moderate. They wanted to turn the party back to a more conservative path and their preferred candidate was the former Hollywood movie star and California Governor Reagan. After an intense battle in the primaries, Ford finally saw off the Reagan challenge, but the vote at the Republican Convention in the summer of 1976 was close: 1,187 votes for Ford and 1,070 for Reagan.

Ford fought a gallant campaign. Considering the political baggage he was carrying — not least the memory of the Nixon pardon — Ford did well to run the Democratic candidate, Governor Jimmy Carter of Georgia, so close. A turning point in the campaign seemed to come during a televised debate between Carter and Ford. Max Frankel of the *New York Times* asked the President a fairly innocuous question on the Helsinki Accord. Having answered the question, Ford — unwisely — pressed on:

> Now, what has been accomplished by the Helsinki agreement? Number one, we have an agreement where they [the Soviet Union] notify us and we notify them of any military manoeuvres that are to be undertaken. They have done it in both cases where they've done so. There is no Soviet domination of Eastern Europe, and there never will be under a Ford Administration.

Frankel, surprised at the final assertion by the President, seemed to offer Ford a chance to withdraw, or at least clarify:

> Did I understand you to say, Sir, that the Russians are not using Eastern Europe as their own sphere of influence and occupying most of the countries there and making sure with their troops that it's a Communist zone?

Ford merely dug deeper:

> I don't believe that the Yugoslavians consider themselves dominated by the Soviet Union. I don't believe the Romanians consider themselves dominated by the Soviet Union. I don't believe the Poles consider themselves dominated by the Soviet Union.

Governor Carter, looking rather pleased with himself, jumped in:

> I'd like to see Mr Ford convince the Polish-Americans and the Czech-Americans and the Hungarian-Americans in this country that those countries don't live under the domination and supervision of the Soviet Union behind the Iron Curtain.

It was one of the great misspeaks of television presidential debates of all time! Ford fell off in the polls and at the election lost by 297 electoral college votes to 241.

An assessment

Making an assessment of such a short presidency — 895 days — is a difficult task. Indeed, Ford's presidency is the fifth shortest in the history of the office, as shown in Table 6.1. The four presidents with shorter tenures all died in office. But how is Ford remembered — as a healer of a divided nation or as an over-promoted failure?

Table 6.1 The ten shortest presidential tenures

President	Days in office
William Harrison (1841)	31
James Garfield (1881)	199
Zachary Taylor (1849–50)	492
Warren Harding (1921–23)	881
Gerald Ford (1974–77)	**895**
Millard Fillmore (1850–53)	968
John Kennedy (1961–63)	1,036
Chester Arthur (1881–85)	1,261
Andrew Johnson (1865–69)	1,419
John Tyler (1841–45)	1,428

The very first assessment was offered by Jimmy Carter, Ford's successor, in the opening sentence of his inaugural address on 20 January 1977. 'For myself and for our nation, I want to thank my predecessor for all he has done to heal our land.' It was a generous tribute, greeted by warm applause.

Henry Kissinger, who served both Nixon and Ford as Secretary of State, offers this assessment of Ford in his biographical volume *Years of Renewal*:

With Ford, what one saw was what one got. Providence smiled on Americans when — seemingly by chance — it brought forward a president who embodied our nation's deepest and simplest values.

Almost three decades later, on the morning following the announcement of Ford's death, President George W. Bush issued a statement from the White House, in which he made this assessment: 'For a nation that needed healing, and for an office that needed a calm and steady hand, Gerald Ford came along when we needed him most.' Later, Bush offered this assessment in his eulogy at the service held in Washington National Cathedral a few days after Ford's death:

> Gerald Ford assumed the presidency when the nation needed a leader of character and humility — and we found it in the man from Grand Rapids. President Ford's time in office was brief, but history will long remember the courage and common sense that helped restore trust in the workings of our democracy.

Dick Cheney, who had served as Ford's Chief of Staff, said that Ford 'embodied the best values of a great generation — decency, integrity and devotion to duty,' adding that 'when he left office, he had restored public trust in the presidency'.

Ford was always modest and self-deprecating about his abilities. After having been sworn into office as vice-president in December 1973, he addressed his former House of Representatives with the line: 'I am a Ford, not a Lincoln,' a reference not only to the heroic president, but to the contrast between the modest Ford cars and the luxury Lincoln. He named his memoirs *A Time to Heal*, and commented in a 1987 interview with the *Harvard Business Review* that 'if I'm remembered, it will probably be for healing the land'.

Ford was in many ways the antithesis of Nixon. Where Nixon was secretive, private and broody, Ford was open, affable and straightforward. Upon hearing that Nixon kept an 'enemies list' in the White House, Ford dryly remarked that 'anybody who can't keep his enemies in his head has too many enemies'. In researching a book on the American presidents' cabinet a decade ago, I interviewed a number of people who served both Nixon and Ford as cabinet members. Even the way the two presidents began a meeting was significantly different. Upon Nixon's arrival, I was told, all the cabinet were expected to jump to their feet and wait to be asked to be seated again. Ford came into the cabinet room and went round shaking cabinet members by the hand, greeting many of them personally. The tone was different.

However, apart from beginning the process of restoring the tarnished image of the presidency, Ford's political achievements were limited. As an unelected president facing a Congress that had, in effect, forced his predecessor to resign, Ford was in a position of great weakness. Ford's 44 regular vetoes and

22 pocket vetoes, delivered in less than 3 years, speak volumes about his relationship with Congress. His response to the worsening economic situation was inept. As presidential scholar Lewis Gould wrote (*The Modern American Presidency*, 2003): 'Such ineffectual gestures as the WIN campaign complete with buttons to "Whip Inflation Now" indicated a gimmicky side to Ford's approach that further eroded the President's credibility.' Gould goes on to comment on the difficult position in which Ford — a moderate Republican — was in:

> Ford found himself between a Democratic Congress determined to scale back presidential power and a Republican Party moving rightward toward Ronald Reagan and the conservatism that flowered in the 1980s.

The Ford administration never really had a 'vision'. There was no 'new deal' or 'new frontier' coming out of the Ford White House. Maybe there just wasn't time, or perhaps Ford simply wasn't a 'vision' person. A noted Ford critic, Adlai Stevenson III, commented in a 1987 interview that Ford had 'no strong views of where the country should be going, no strong understanding of history and the world'. Another presidential scholar, John Robert Greene (*The Presidency of Gerald R. Ford*, 1995), wrote that 'the administration did not have an agenda mainly because there was little time to think of one'. Most presidents have an election campaign followed by a 2-month transition period to draw up their policy agenda. Ford came to office with no warning, no team and no agenda. If Nixon had personified the so-called 'imperial presidency', then Ford — and Carter — personified the 'imperilled presidency', a term that Ford was the first to use, in an article in *Time* magazine in November 1980.

Perhaps in August 1974 the nation merely wanted honesty and tranquillity, not brilliance or vision. And although Ford had to some extent 'restored much of the lustre to a badly tarnished presidency, one could not conclude that at the end of his tenure the nation had fully regained trust in its government' (John Robert Greene). Ford used to like to quote President Harry Truman's self-evaluation: 'He had guts, he was plain-talking, he had no illusions about being a great intellectual, but he seemed to make the right decisions.' In a 2005 ranking of American presidents, Gerald Ford was judged as 'below average', coming in at number 28 out of the 40 presidents ranked. He was ranked lower than Lyndon Johnson (18th) and Bill Clinton (22nd), but above Richard Nixon (32nd) and Jimmy Carter (34th) — a healer, not a *great* president, but no failure either.

In their study of presidential performance published in 2000 (*The American Presidents Ranked by Performance*), Charles and Richard Faber wrote:

> Ford restored to the office of the president some of the respect that it had lost both at home and abroad because of the actions of his predecessor. He had a reputation for integrity and trustworthiness. His personal morality stood in

such a marked contrast to that of certain other presidents that it enhanced the prestige of the office of the president.

In Gerald Ford Americans got, in the words of one Ford White House staffer, 'a solid, simple, honest, decent man'. There are times in a nation's history when people are happy to settle for that.

Questions

1 Briefly trace Gerald Ford's political career, from his entry to the House of Representatives in 1948 to his becoming president in 1974.
2 Why did Gerald Ford have only a brief 'honeymoon' as president?
3 Assess whether Ford's decision to pardon Nixon was the right decision to have made.
4 Why was 1975 such a politically bleak year for President Ford?
5 How did Ford get himself into difficulties in a television debate with Jimmy Carter in the 1976 election campaign?
6 What did Ford mean when he declared in 1973: 'I'm a Ford, not a Lincoln'?
7 What were the main strengths and weaknesses of the Ford presidency?

Chapter 7

Congressional elections 2008

What you need to know

- Congressional elections are held every 2 years.
- These elections are for the whole of the House of Representatives and one third of the Senate.
- There are 435 members of the House and 100 members of the Senate.
- House members serve 2-year terms. Senators serve 6-year terms.
- Since the 2006 mid-term elections, the Democrats have been the majority party in both houses of Congress.

The elections to be held on 4 November 2008 will not only determine the control of the White House but also that of Congress. Since 2006, the Democrats have enjoyed a small majority in both houses: a two-seat majority in the Senate and a 31-seat majority in the House. Therefore, the Republicans would need to make an overall gain of two seats to be sure of retaking control of the Senate. (If they retain the White House, a one-seat gain would be sufficient, with the Vice-President casting the tie-breaking vote.) To retake control of the House of Representatives, the Republicans need an overall gain of at least 16 seats. Both of these scenarios seem unlikely. Indeed, what seems far more likely is that the Democrats will further increase their majorities in both houses. In this chapter, we shall try to discover the extent of the likely Democrat gains and the reasons why they may occur.

Senate races

Going into the 2008 elections, the party balance in the Senate is 49–49, with two independents. But as both independents — Joe Lieberman of Connecticut and Bernie Sanders of Vermont — side with the Democrats, the Democrats have an effective 51 to 49-seat majority. Of the 34 seats up for re-election, the Republicans are defending 22 and the Democrats only 12. That gives the Democrats a huge advantage.

Another reason for Democrat optimism is that these seats were last contested in 2002 when President Bush was at the height of his popularity following

9/11. Republican candidates did unexpectedly well, winning seats that they would normally have thought to be out of their grasp. In 2008, with a weakened, unpopular, lame duck Republican president and possibly not a strong presidential candidate for 2008, the Democrats will presume that the wind is at their backs this time around. A further reason for Democrat optimism is that, at the time of writing, all 12 incumbent Democrat senators were running for re-election (see Table 7.1). Thus, the Democrats will have no open seats to defend. Open seats are almost always more difficult to defend than those in which an incumbent is running for re-election.

Table 7.1 Democrat Senators seeking re-election in 2008

Senator	State	Percentage of vote (2002)
John Kerry	Massachusetts	80
Jack Reed	Rhode Island	78
Max Baucus	Montana	63
John Rockefeller	West Virginia	63
Carl Levin	Michigan	61
Richard Durbin	Illinois	60
Joseph Biden	Delaware	58
Mark Pryor	Arkansas	54
Tom Harkin	Iowa	54
Frank Lautenberg	New Jersey	54
Mary Landrieu	Louisiana	52
Tim Johnson	South Dakota	50

In contrast, the Republicans already have a number of incumbent senators who have decided not to seek re-election in 2008: Wayne Allard of Colorado, Larry Craig of Idaho, Chuck Hagel of Nebraska, Pete Domenici of New Mexico and John Warner of Virginia have all announced retirement plans, and others may yet follow. The Democrats seem to have a real prospect of picking up three or more of these open seats (see Table 7.2).

Colorado is a state that is becoming increasingly Democratic. In 2004, the Democrats picked up the other Colorado Senate seat following the retirement of Republican Ben Nighthorse Campbell. Democrats now control four of the state's seven House seats. Pete Domenici would probably have been a shoo-in if he had run for a seventh term in New Mexico, but without Domenici's name on the ballot, the Democrats may pick up a seat in the state that George W. Bush won by only a whisker in 2004. The same story is true of Virginia, where John Warner has declined to seek a sixth term. The Democrats have a strong candidate in Mark Warner (no relation), the former Governor of the state.

Table 7.2 Senators grouped by class showing date of next election

Class 2 (next election 2008)	Class 3 (next election 2010)	Class 1 (next election 2012)
Alabama: Jeff Sessions (R)	Alabama: Richard Shelby (R)	Arizona: John Kyl (R)
Alaska: Ted Stevens (R)	Alaska: Lisa Murkowski (R)	California: Dianne Feinstein (D)
Arkansas: Mark Pryor (D)	Arizona: John McCain (R)	Connecticut: Joe Lieberman (I)
Colorado: Wayne Allard (R)	Arkansas: Blanche Lincoln (D)	Delaware: Thomas Carper (D)
Delaware: Joe Biden (D)	California: Barbara Boxer (D)	Florida: Bill Nelson (D)
Georgia: Saxby Chambliss (R)	Colorado: Ken Salazar (D)	Hawaii: Daniel Akaka (D)
Idaho: Larry Craig (R)	Connecticut: Christopher Dodd (D)	Indiana: Richard Lugar (R)
Illinois: Richard Durbin (D)	Florida: Mel Martinez (R)	Maine: Olympia Snowe (R)
Iowa: Tom Harkin (D)	Georgia: Johnny Isakson (R)	Maryland: Benjamin Cardin (D)
Kansas: Pat Roberts (R)	Hawaii: Daniel Inouye (D)	Massachusetts: Edward Kennedy (D)
Kentucky: Mitch McConnell (R)	Idaho: Mike Crapo (R)	Michigan: Debbie Stabenow (D)
Louisiana: Mary Landrieu (D)	Illinois: Barack Obama (D)	Minnesota: Amy Klobuchar (D)
Maine: Susan Collins (R)	Indiana: Evan Bayh (D)	Mississippi: Trent Lott (R)
Massachusetts: John Kerry (D)	Iowa: Charles Grassley (R)	Missouri: Claire McCaskill (D)
Michigan: Carl Levin (D)	Kansas: Sam Brownback (R)	Montana: Jon Tester (D)
Minnesota: Norm Coleman (R)	Kentucky: Jim Bunning (R)	Nebraska: Ben Nelson (D)
Mississippi: Thad Cochran (R)	Louisiana: David Vitter (R)	Nevada: John Ensign (R)
Montana: Max Baucus (D)	Maryland: Barbara Mikulski (D)	New Jersey: Robert Menendez (D)
Nebraska: Chuck Hagel (R)	Missouri: Christopher Bond (R)	New Mexico: Jeff Bingaman (D)
New Hampshire: John Sununu (R)	Nevada: Harry Reid (D)	New York: Hillary Clinton (D)
New Jersey: Frank Lautenberg (D)	New Hampshire: Judd Gregg (R)	North Dakota: Kent Conrad (D)
New Mexico: Pete Domenici (R)	New York: Charles Schumer (D)	Ohio: Sherrod Brown (D)
North Carolina: Elizabeth Dole (R)	North Carolina: Richard Burr (R)	Pennsylvania: Robert Casey (D)
Oklahoma: James Inhofe (R)	North Dakota: Byron Dorgan (D)	Rhode Island: Sheldon Whitehouse (D)
Oregon: Gordon Smith (R)	Ohio: George Voinovich (R)	Tennessee: Bob Corker (R)
Rhode Island: Jack Reed (D)	Oklahoma: Tom Coburn (R)	Texas: Kay Bailey Hutchison (R)
South Carolina: Lindsey Graham (R)	Oregon: Ron Wyden (D)	Utah: Orrin Hatch (R)
South Dakota: Tim Johnson (D)	Pennsylvania: Arlen Specter (R)	Vermont: Bernie Sanders (I)
Tennessee: Lamar Alexander (R)	South Carolina: Jim DeMint (R)	Virginia: Jim Webb (D)
Texas: John Cornyn (R)	South Dakota: John Thune (R)	Washington: Maria Cantwell (D)
Virginia: John Warner (R)	Utah: Robert Bennett (R)	West Virginia: Robert Byrd (D)
West Virginia: John Rockefeller (D)	Vermont: Patrick Leahy (D)	Wisconsin: Herb Kohl (D)
Wyoming: Michael Enzi (R)	Washington: Patty Murray (D)	Wyoming: John Barrasso (R)
	Wisconsin: Russell Feingold (D)	
21 Republicans (R)	**19 Republicans (R)**	**9 Republicans (R)**
12 Democrats (D)	**15 Democrats (D)**	**22 Democrats (D)**
	2 Independents (I)	

There are two potentially vulnerable Republican incumbents who the Democrats would hope to defeat: Norm Coleman of Minnesota and John Sununu of New Hampshire (see Table 7.3). Both states were won by the Democrat candidate John Kerry in the 2004 presidential race and both Coleman and Sununu were elected with very small majorities back in 2002. Coleman's Democratic challenger could be radio talk show host Al Franken, while Sununu will probably face New Hampshire's popular former Governor Jeanne Shaheen.

In Maine, Susan Collins faces a strong challenge from six-term Democrat Congressman Tom Allen. Scandal-tarnished Ted Stevens faces the possibility of a primary challenge in Alaska, as does Lindsey Graham in South Carolina. At the turn of 2008, of the 22 seats being defended by the Republicans, only nine of them (Mississippi, Kansas, Wyoming, Kentucky, Alabama, Oklahoma, Texas, Tennessee and Georgia) appeared certain to remain in the Republican column. No wonder the Democrats think they are in with a chance of more substantial gains in the Senate this time around.

Table 7.3 Republican Senators seeking re-election in 2008

Senator	State	Percentage of vote (2002)
Thad Cochran	Mississippi	85
Pat Roberts	Kansas	83
Ted Stevens	Alaska	78
Mike Enzi	Wyoming	73
Mitch McConnell	Kentucky	64
Jeff Sessions	Alabama	59
Susan Collins	Maine	58
James Inhofe	Oklahoma	57
Gordon Smith	Oregon	56
John Cornyn	Texas	55
Elizabeth Dole	North Carolina	54
Lindsey Graham	South Carolina	54
Lamar Alexander	Tennessee	54
Saxby Chambliss	Georgia	53
John Sununu	New Hampshire	51
Norm Coleman	Minnesota	50
John Barrasso	Wyoming	*

*John Barrasso was appointed in 2007 following the death of Senator Craig Thomas (R). In 2008, Barrasso will be seeking election to serve out the remaining 4 years of Thomas's term.

This is not to say that the Democrats don't have any concerns of their own. There are a couple of Democrat-controlled Senate seats that appear vulnerable.

In South Dakota in 2002, Tim Johnson won by only 524 votes. Between December 2006 and April 2007, Senator Johnson spent 4 months in hospital after a brain haemorrhage and he returned to the Senate only in September 2007 after a 9-month absence. If the Republicans could field a strong candidate, they would fancy their chances of winning the seat.

Another Democrat-controlled Senate seat that the Republicans have on their hit-list is Mary Landrieu's seat in Louisiana. Landrieu won re-election to her second term in 2002 with just 52% of the vote. As a result of Hurricane Katrina, many black Americans have been displaced from New Orleans, with large numbers dispersed to neighbouring states, and thus the natural Democrat vote in the state has declined. Landrieu's difficulties were further compounded in August 2007 when the popular State Treasurer John Kennedy announced he was switching parties from the Democrats to the Republicans. The rumour was that Kennedy's party switch was a precursor to a challenge for Landrieu's Senate seat in 2008. Louisiana has become increasingly Republican in recent elections. In 2004, Bush won the state in the presidential election by 15 percentage points, while at the same time the state elected a Republican Senator — David Vitter — for the first time since the Civil War. In October 2007, Bobby Jindal won the state governorship for the Republicans.

The only other Senate Democrat incumbent with an eye to defeat is freshman Mark Pryor of Arkansas. But unless Mike Huckabee (the popular former Republican Governor of the state) abandons his presidential bid and settles instead for challenging Pryor, the Democrat should hold on comfortably.

The likely outcome in the Senate is for the Democrats to make a gain of between three and six seats; however, that would leave them well short of the 60-vote filibuster-proof majority for which parties crave.

House races

Going into the 2008 elections, the party balance in the House of Representatives is likely to be 233 Democrats and 202 Republicans. It seems almost inconceivable that the Republicans could pull off a gain of 16 seats to win back their majority in the House. What seems more likely is that the Republicans will lose ground to the Democrats, and they are likely to begin the 111th Congress in January 2009 with fewer than 200 House members for the first time in 16 years.

Of the 435 House races, only 34 were being ranked as truly competitive by the Cook Political Report (see **www.cookpolitical.com**) in mid-October 2007: 14 Democrat-held seats and 20 Republican-held seats. There are another 17 Republican-held seats that could be vulnerable if the Republicans have a truly awful election. The seats in most danger for the Republicans are those where popular incumbents are retiring: Rick Renzi in Arizona, Jerry Weller in Illinois, Jim Ramsted in Minnesota, Deborah Pryce in Ohio and Heather Wilson, who is running for the open Senate seat in New Mexico.

Other vulnerable Republican House members are the eight who sit in districts won by Democrat Senator John Kerry in 2004 (see Table 7.4). After the 2004 elections, there were 18 Republican House members in Districts won by John Kerry. Ten of those 18 lost their re-election bids in 2006. The Democrats will be hoping to make further inroads into the 'Kerry Republicans' in 2008.

Table 7.4 Republican House members elected in districts that voted for John Kerry (D) in 2004

District	Bush vote in District in 2004 (%)	House member
Delaware (At Large)	45.8	Mike Castle
Connecticut 4	46.3	Christopher Shays
Illinois 10	47.2	Mark Kirk
New Mexico 1	47.8	*Heather Wilson
New York 25	47.8	Jim Walsh
Washington 8	48.1	Dave Reichert
Pennsylvania 6	48.2	Jim Gerlach
Pennsylvania 15	49.6	Charlie Dent

*Running for vacant Senate seat in 2008

There is one Democrat incumbent whose future is far from guaranteed: Baron Hill in Indiana's 9th district. Hill defeated incumbent Republican Mike Sodrel in 2002, despite the Republican having spent more that $1 million of his own money on the race. But in 2004, Sodrel won the seat back, only to lose it again to Hill in 2006. Sodrel has announced that he will be back to challenge the seat again in 2008, so it is worth looking out for Round IV in the Sodrel versus Hill grudge match in Indiana. But all in all, it looks like a Democrat Congress after the 2008 elections.

There was one ray of sunshine for Republican candidates as 2007 drew to a close. In a special election to fill the remaining term of retired Massachusetts House Democrat Martin Meehan, the Republican candidate came within 6 percentage points of winning the seat. The Democrat winner was Nicola Tsongas, the widow of the late Massachusetts Senator Paul Tsongas, who outspent her opponent by more than four to one. Her husband had even represented the same District before his election to the Senate. Yet the Republican candidate, farmer and businessman Jim Ogonowski, got 45% of the vote with a vigorous anti-Washington campaign. Ogonowski tied Tsongas to what he claimed was the failed politics of the Democrat-controlled Congress in Washington. The effect seemed to be impressive. In 2006, Meehan had won re-election unopposed and even in 2004 had seen off his Republican opponent by 34 percentage points: 67–33. What Republicans must hope for is that, by blaming the Democrats for the failures of the past 2 years, they can avoid losing too much ground to them in 2008.

Postscript: 2012 and beyond

Attention is already turning to the reapportionment of House seats, which will take place as a result of the decennial census in 2010. Based on the state population figures produced by that census, the allocation of House seats to a number of states will need to be adjusted up or down. Going on projected figures, there is already some indication as to which states may be the winners and losers.

There are eight states on track to gain House seats. Texas could gain up to four new House seats, Arizona and Florida could gain two each, while Georgia, Nevada, Oregon, Utah and Washington are likely to gain one new seat. As Table 7.5 shows, six of these eight states already return a majority of Republicans to the House of Representatives; only Oregon returns a majority of Democrats, while the Arizona House delegation is currently evenly divided. In four of the eight states, the Republicans also currently control the state governorship as well as both houses in the state legislature. This is true for the Democrats in only two states — Oregon and Washington.

Table 7.5 States likely to gain House seats in 2012

State	Likely gains in House seats	Current House delegation (Dem–Rep)	Party currently controlling		
			Governor	State Senate	State House
Texas	+4	13–19	R	R	R
Arizona	+2	4–4	D	R	R
Florida	+2	9–16	R	R	R
Georgia	+1	6–7	R	R	R
Nevada	+1	1–2	R	R	D
Oregon	+1	4–1	D	D	D
Utah	+1	1–2	R	R	R
Washington	+1	3–6	D	D	D

This information about party control of state government is relevant and important because, in most states, it is the state government that is responsible for drawing up the new congressional district boundaries. In a few states, this task is given to a non-partisan commission. Of the eight states in Table 7.5,

only Arizona uses a non-partisan commission to draw up its congressional district boundaries. Thus, party control of the state government is another important ingredient in assessing the likely outcome of any redistribution of House seats.

There are 11 states that are likely to lose House seats (Table 7.6). New York and Ohio are likely to lose two seats each, while the states that may lose one seat are Illinois, Iowa, Louisiana, Massachusetts, Michigan, Minnesota, Missouri, New Jersey and Pennsylvania. As Table 7.6 shows, seven of these 11 states currently return a majority of Democrats to the House of Representatives; only Ohio, Louisiana, Michigan and Missouri return a majority of Republicans to the House. In five of the 11 states, the Democrats currently control the state governorship as well as both houses in the state legislature. This is true for the Republicans in only one state: Missouri.

Table 7.6 States likely to lose House seats in 2012

State	Likely losses in House seats	Current House delegation (Dem–Rep)	Party currently controlling		
			Governor	State Senate	State House
New York	−2	23–6	D	R	D
Ohio	−2	7–11	D	R	R
Illinois	−1	10–9	D	D	D
Iowa	−1	3–2	D	D	D
Louisiana	−1	2–5	D	D	D
Massachusetts	−1	10–0	D	D	D
Michigan	−1	6–9	D	R	D
Minnesota	−1	5–3	R	D	D
Missouri	−1	4–5	R	R	R
New Jersey	−1	7–6	D	D	D
Pennsylvania	−1	11–8	D	R	D

Changes in the allocation of House seats for these states will also mean changes in their Electoral College votes. If these changes were to go ahead, the consequences in the Electoral College would be of advantage to the Republicans by between 5 and 10 votes from 2012. Generally speaking, it is red (Republican) states — Texas, Arizona, Georgia, Utah and the like — that are gaining extra votes, while blue (Democrat) states — such as New York, Illinois, New Jersey and Pennsylvania — are losing votes. If the 2004 election had been fought on these figures, George W. Bush would have won in the Electoral College Vote not by 286–252 but by 292–246.

Questions

1 Explain why the Democrats are likely to gain between three and six seats in the Senate in 2008.

2 After 2004, there were 18 House Republicans who represented districts won by Democrat John Kerry in the 2004 presidential election. What has happened to those 18 House Republicans and what may occur in 2008? Give examples.

3 Why did the result of the special election in Massachusetts in 2007 offer 'a ray of sunshine' for Republican candidates?

4 Use an internet search engine to find out more about the Republican candidate in the Massachusetts election, Jim Ogonowski. What did you discover about his brother, John, and how might this have had an impact on the race?

5 Why might the reapportionment of House seats after the 2010 census be good news for Republicans?

Who's who in US politics 2008

Executive branch

President	George W. Bush
Vice-President	Dick Cheney

The cabinet

Secretary of State	Condoleezza Rice
Secretary of Defense	Robert Gates
Secretary of the Treasury	Henry Paulson
Secretary of Agriculture	Ed Schafer
Secretary of the Interior	Dirk Kempthorne
Attorney General (Justice Department)	Michael Mukasey
Secretary of Commerce	Carlos Gutierrez
Secretary of Labor	Elaine Chao
Secretary of Health and Human Services	Michael Leavitt
Secretary of Education	Margaret Spellings
Secretary of Housing and Urban Development	Alphonso Jackson
Secretary of Transportation	Mary Peters
Secretary of Energy	Samuel Bodman
Secretary of Veterans' Affairs	James Peake
Secretary of Homeland Security	Michael Chertoff

Executive Office of the President personnel

White House Chief of Staff	Joshua Bolten
Director of Office of Management and Budget	Jim Nussle
National Security Adviser	Stephen Hadley
Chairman of Council of Economic Advisers	Edward Lazear
Assistant to the President for Legislative Affairs	Candida Wolff
Trade Representative	Susan Schwab
Administrator of Environmental Protection Agency	Stephen Johnson
Press Secretary	Dana Perino

Other executive branch personnel

Director of Central Intelligence Agency (CIA)	General Michael Hayden
Director of Federal Bureau of Investigation (FBI)	Robert Mueller
Chairman of the Joint Chiefs of Staff (JCS)	Admiral Michael Mullen

Legislative branch

President *Pro Tempore* of the Senate	Robert Byrd (D–West Virginia)
Senate Majority Leader	Harry Reid (D–Nevada)
Senate Minority Leader	Mitch McConnell (R–Kentucky)
Senate Majority Whip	Richard Durbin (D–Illinois)
Senate Minority Whip	Jon Kyl (R–Arizona)
Speaker of the House of Representatives	Nancy Pelosi (D–California)
House Majority Leader	Steny Hoyer (D–Maryland)
House Minority Leader	John Boehner (R–Ohio)
House Majority Whip	James Clyburn (D–South Carolina)
House Minority Whip	Roy Blunt (R–Missouri)

Senate Standing Committee chairs

Agriculture, Nutrition and Forestry	Tom Harkin	Iowa
Appropriations	Robert Byrd	West Virginia
Armed Services	Carl Levin	Michigan
Banking, Housing and Urban Affairs	Christopher Dodd	Connecticut
Budget	Kent Conrad	North Dakota
Commerce, Science and Transportation	Daniel Inouye	Hawaii
Energy and Natural Resources	Jeff Bingaman	New Mexico
Environment and Public Works	Barbara Boxer	California
Finance	Max Baucus	Montana
Foreign Relations	Joseph Biden	Maryland
Health, Education, Labor and Pensions	Edward Kennedy	Massachusetts
Homeland Security and Governmental Affairs	Joseph Lieberman	Connecticut
Judiciary	Patrick Leahy	Vermont
Rules and Administration	Dianne Feinstein	California
Small Business and Entrepreneurship	John Kerry	Massachusetts
Veterans' Affairs	Daniel Akaka	Hawaii

House Standing Committee chairs

Agriculture	Collin Peterson	Minnesota
Appropriations	David Obey	Wisconsin
Armed Services	Ike Skelton	Missouri
Budget	John Spratt	South Carolina
Education and Labor	George Miller	California
Energy and Commerce	John Dingell	Michigan
Financial Services	Barney Frank	Massachusetts
Foreign Affairs	Tom Lantos	California
Homeland Security	Bennie Thompson	Mississippi
Judiciary	John Conyers	Michigan

Natural Resources	Nick Rahall	West Virginia
Oversight and Government Reform	Henry Waxman	California
Rules	Louise Slaughter	New York
Science and Technology	Bart Gordon	Tennessee
Small Business	Nydia Velázquez	New York
Transportation and Infrastructure	James Oberstar	Minnesota
Veterans' Affairs	Bob Filner	California
Ways and Means	Charles Rangel	New York

Judicial branch

		President who appointed	Year appointed
Chief Justice	John Roberts	George W. Bush	2005
Associate Justices	John Paul Stevens	Ford	1975
	Antonin Scalia	Reagan	1986
	Anthony Kennedy	Reagan	1987
	David Souter	Bush	1990
	Clarence Thomas	Bush	1991
	Ruth Bader Ginsburg	Clinton	1993
	Stephen Breyer	Clinton	1994
	Samuel Alito	George W. Bush	2006